KAGYU SAMYE LING

THE STORY

KAGYU SAMYE LING
THE STORY

With gratitude for the generous support of the INLIGHT Trust

Books available online from the Samye Ling shop at www.samyelingshop.com

Dzalendara Publishing
Rokpa Trust
Kagyu Samye Ling Monestary and Tibetan Centre
Eskdalemuir, Dumfriesshire DG13 0QL Scotland UK
Tel: +44 (0)13873 73232   Fax: +44 (0)13873 73223
Email: scotland@samyeling.org   www.samye.org

Front cover photo by J.W. Emmerson
Back cover photo by Anna Branthwaite

Design, Layout & Printing by Print Graphic Ltd - 01228 593900

ISBN: 0906181-23-2

Please note: all proceeds from the sale of this book will go towards the
realisation of Akong Tulku Rinpoche's vision to complete the Samye Project
with the building of Phase III

Namo

Homage to His Holiness the XVIIth Gyalwa Karmapa
Urgyen Trinley Dorje, Supreme Head of the Kagyu Lineage,
To Choje Akong Tulku Rinpoche, Lama Yeshe Losal Rinpoche
And to all the glorious Masters of the precious Lineages

Please accept this little book as an offering dedicated in
Your honour, with prayers for your long and fruitful lives,
That your Buddha activity may continue to flourish
For the benefit and happiness of all sentient beings

LONDON SW1A OPW

FOREWORD

This is a remarkable book describing both the physical development of the Samye Ling monastery and its spiritual development and outreach.

I first visited the original temple (lovingly described) soon after it opened in 1967 together with my old friends Lord and Lady Tanlaw who as residents in Eskdale were very supportive of the venture when not everybody locally was.

I was impressed and returned several times, and was both honoured and delighted to officiate at the opening of the new temple in 1988, and later at the inauguration of Phase 2 by His Holiness the Dalai Lama (whom I have recently visited in Dharamsala). I also went with Akong Rinpoche and Lama Yeshe to Holy Island at its inauguration – a place of tangible spirituality, and called again a couple of years later when the derelict houses had been restored.

The contribution which the Tibetan Buddhist community has made to these two places in Scotland is enormous, not just in their economic development but in the help they have given to individuals, and in the whole ethos which they represent.

David Steel   March 2007

ACKNOWLEDGEMENTS

When Akong Tulku Rinpoche first asked me, in August 2006, to compile and write a book on Samye Ling's history in time for the 40th anniversary in 2007 my initial surprise was succeded by a mixture of delight and apprehension. What to write? Where to find research materials? Who to speak to? How long should the book be? etc.etc. In answer Akong Rinpoche simply said, "Just do whatever you have time for".

Keeping his advice in mind and knowing that there would only be five months in which to accomplish the task alongside many other commitments, necessitated a pragmatic approach of speaking to a limited cross section of people who were representative of the various decades and activities at Samye Ling over the years. Had there been more time at my disposal it would have been possible to talk to many other equally knowledgeable people with similarly fascinating insights. Their absence from the narrative in no way reflects on their contribution to Samye Ling's development but was merely a practical matter of there simply not being enough time to contact everyone. Nonetheless I apologise for being unable to mention many deserving people and for any omissions or mistakes made in the telling of Samye Ling's story.

I am most grateful to all the people who helped bring the story alive through their personal reminiscences. Thanks in particular to Sherab Palden Beru, Lama Zangmo, Ani Tsultrim Zangmo, Joyce Armstrong, Mamie Bannerman, Harry Milward, Ken and Katia Holmes, Dolma Jeffries, Carol Sagar, Rob Nairn, Edie Irwin, Lea Wyler, Vin and Marilyn Harris, Bernard Provost, Sue Bradley, Marian Dreyfus and George Briggs, all of whom were most generous with their time, memories and invaluable information. Thanks also to Penelope for typing all the lists in the back section of the book, and to Ani Tsultrim Wangmo for her painstaking photo scanning.

Finally I wish to express my deepest gratitude to Akong Tulku Rinpoche and Lama Yeshe Losal Rinpoche without whom I would never have had the opportunity, or indeed the courage to attempt this daunting project. The resulting book is the best I could do in the time available, though it is really only the tip of a considerably larger iceberg. Nevertheless, hopefully it goes some way towards fulfilling Akong Rinpoche's request and gives the reader an idea of the truly amazing story of Samye Ling.

My heartfelt prayer is that Akong Tulku Rinpoche and Lama Yeshe Rinpoche will live long and healthy lives and continue to help countless people through their Buddha activity at Samye Ling and around the world.

Ani Rinchen Khandro
Samye Ling, February 2007

Dorje Chang, the primordial Buddha, by Sherab Palden Beru

CONTENTS

CHAPTER I

SEEDS OF CHANGE

Kagyu Samye Ling Monastery was the first and is the largest Centre of Tibetan Buddhism and Culture in Europe. As one travels through the softly undulating hills of southern Scotland, the surprise and delight at suddenly glimpsing Samye Ling's magnificent temple and stupa, with their glinting copper roofs and steeple bedecked by fluttering prayer flags, is like that of finding a rare species of orchid in the midst of a Scottish meadow. To discover how such an exotic bloom came to flourish in the beautiful but unlikely setting of the Esk valley requires a journey back in time and space to 1950's Tibet.

The story begins in Tibet's eastern province of Kham where two young Lamas, namely Akong Tulku Rinpoche and Chogyam Trungpa Rinpoche, lived and presided over their respective monasteries of Dolma Lhakang and Surmang. As tulkus, or reincarnate Lamas, each of the young Abbots was treated with great veneration, not only by the ordained sangha of their monasteries, but also by the thousands of lay people in their areas who would look to them for guidance in matters of importance to their lives.

According to Tibetan Buddhism a tulku is an enlightened being who acts with wisdom and compassion to relieve the suffering of others and guide them to realisation of their true nature. They are given the title of Rinpoche, which means precious, great being. When such holy ones die they are able to choose favourable circumstances for their next rebirth so that they can continue their work. Therefore, when such children are recognised as tulkus they are treated as living emanations of the Lord Buddha. Among Tibetans it is a tremendous honour to have a tulku in their family and they would be happy and proud to allow the child to be raised and trained by the monastery.

Both Akong Tulku Rinpoche and Chogyam Trungpa Rinpoche were recognised as tulkus in their early childhood by the then head of the Kagyu Lineage, His Holiness the 16th Gyalwa Karmapa. They were duly enthroned in their monasteries and received the traditional monastic training that enabled them to become Abbots and assume responsibility for their monasteries and for the spiritual welfare of many thousands of monks, nuns and lay devotees. Although their monasteries were situated in remote regions of Tibet, and were undoubtedly austere by modern European standards, nevertheless the two Rinpoches enjoyed comfortable and privileged lives with their every need catered for by retinues of devoted monks.

The tulkus had known each other since they were fourteen years old and Akong Rinpoche had travelled to Surmang to receive the Rinchen Tertsog initiation from Trungpa when they were both just fifteen. Indeed, their previous incarnations, the first Akong Tulku and the tenth Chogyam Trungpa had also been close and had given each other teachings when visiting the other's monastery. Although Surmang was a ten day ride on horseback from Dolma Lhakang the two monastries had a long association going back several centuries and, by Tibetan standards, were considered geographically as well as spiritually close.

In 1957 Akong Rinpoche left Dolma Lhakang in order to receive individual instructions, including the profound Mahamudra teachings, over several months from the great Lama Sechen Kongtrul at Sechen Monastery. Later that year he travelled on to Palpung Monastery to join Trungpa Rinpoche and a number of other Kagyu Lamas in order to receive very special teachings and empowerments from His Holiness the 16th Karmapa. Akong Tulku then returned to Sechen to resume his studies and was later joined by Trungpa Rinpoche before departing together for Surmang. It was during this visit that Akong Rinpoche received many instructions and initiations from Rolpe Dorje Rinpoche, including all the initiations for the three year retreat practices. He also received the very esoteric Demchog Tsogar initiation from Trungpa Rinpoche. Tsogar is a speciality of the Tsurmang tradition which is only given to lineage holders. This particular ceremony only takes place after Losar, Tibetan New Year, which is followed by seven days of Korlo Demchog prayers and concludes with the twenty four hour long Tsogar Initiation featuring sacred dances and a ritual feast. It was 1958 by the time Akong Rinpoche left Surmang to return to his own monastery. En route to Dolma Lhakang he paid a brief visit to his parents at their family home. Little did he know, as he bade them farewell, that he would never see them again.

In 1959 when the young Lamas were still both only nineteen years old they received reports that the Chinese presence in Tibet was becoming increasingly political. The Cultural Revolution's Army began to occupy towns and villages in the east of Tibet, creating waves of Tibetan refugees flowing from east to west. As heads of their monasteries the Rinpoches were prime targets and, knowing that their lives were in danger, reluctantly made hurried preparations for their escape. There was really no choice. Trungpa Rinpoche left Surmang and arrived at Akong Rinpoche's Monastery of Dolma Lhakang as a refugee with a large retinue of monks. From there the Rinpoches and their followers joined forces and, as they travelled towards Lhasa by horseback and pack mules, their group was augmented by others desperate to escape so that their party finally numbered some three hundred people. Among them were Akong Rinpoche's two brothers. The elder brother was Jamyang Chogyal and the younger was fifteen year old Jampal Drakpa, (later to become Lama Yeshe Rinpoche), who had been living at Dolma Lhakang whilst being educated to help with its administration. Akong Rinpoche had thought his parents and the rest of his family would also be joining them, but alas they were prevented by the army.

The escapees took enough food and supplies for what they calculated would be a three month long journey. As the party neared Lhasa it became apparent that the military had taken control of the capital, thus forcing the travellers to find an alternative route of escape. What followed was month after month of arduous journey in ever more difficult conditions. The summer weather gave way to autumn, then to winter as the weary band made their way across innumerable high mountain passes, through ice and snow, often with little or no idea of where they were within Tibet's vast landscape, other than a rough idea of travelling in the direction of India.

After four months of travelling on horseback, their perilous path over increasingly rough terrain meant they had to abandon their animals and much of their baggage in order to cross rivers in full spate, often with nothing more than a narrow, flimsy rope bridge swinging between them and the raging waters below. On reaching the far side the young and old struggled to climb sheer rock faces with only rough hewn footholds to cling to as they hauled themselves up. They calculated that the rest of their journey would take another three months on foot. In fact it took twice as long.

Food supplies dwindled and the hungry travellers were eventually reduced to boiling their yak skin leather bags and belts to chew and extract some little nourishment to sustain themseves in the freezing conditions as they slowly plodded on. Keeping to the high ground they would sometimes see villages, often occupied by soldiers, consequently they would travel mainly at night and sleep during the day hiding under rocks ot trees or wherever they could find cover. Military planes would fly overhead so the group were often unable to light fires in case of detection. Realizing they would soon have to cross the Brahmaputra river, whose boat crossing point was patrolled by soldiers, the travellers took shelter in a forest and set about making coracles out of yak skin and tree resin.

Jettisoning all but the most basic supplies the travellers waited till nightfall then prepared to take to the water by the light of the full moon. The Rinpoches boarded their coracle taking a few treasured, golden, religious relics, which they wore under their robes. The ever practical Jampal Drakpa managed to salvage a kettle and some tea. Some years later Akong Rinpoche reflected that his younger brother had shown more wisdom, as the hot tea had saved their lives on more than one occasion. As dawn broke the first coracle in which the Rinpoches were sailing, made it safely to the other side then the others started to follow but the occupying forces got wind of the escape and started shooting at the people in the coracles. Some were killed but the majority were captured and taken to a prison camp.

Nine of the captives, including Akong Rinpoche's elder brother Jamyang Chogyal, managed to escape from the camp. They caught up with the Rinpoche's party and continued on the most harrowing part of their journey, travelling on foot for a total of six months. Verging on collapse they finally found a cave in which to shelter where, crippled with fatigue and hunger, they crawled inside to sleep.

Unbeknown to the exhausted travellers, they were actually only a few days away from the Indian border. Akong Rinpoche remembers reflecting on how they were still wearing precious relics and jewellery but had nothing to eat or drink so they were waiting to die, decorated with useless riches.

"For the first time I realised that wealth meant nothing and that as human beings we first need something to eat and somewhere to sleep. Luckily we were not meant to die but just be taught a lesson. We were found by some hunters who took us to their village and fed us until we were strong enough to carry on to India. It was this experience which first made me want to help others avoid the sufferings of hunger and homelessness."

Of the three hundred people in the group that left Tibet in April 1959, only fifteen made it to India. Having spent four months on horseback followed by six months on foot to finally reach the Indian border in December the fifteen survivors were exausted, emaciated but alive. The rest of their party had either died from exhaustion and hunger or had been killed or captured along the way.

At the border the Rinpoches and their much reduced group were flown in a military cargo plane to a large refugee camp in Assam. It was there that they first met the Camp Commandant, an extraordinary English woman called Freda Bedi who was to play such a pivotal role in their lives. The refugee camp in Assam was only a temporary holding place from which the refugees would be taken to other camps. Chogyam Trungpa and his Surmang monks went to Kalimpong while Akong Rinpoche, together with his two brothers and the remaining group members were taken to a camp in Buxadaur to join many other Rinpoches who were already living there. The Buxaduar refugee camp had formerly been a British military prison camp and was situated in one of the hottest parts of India where even the tarmac melts on the roads. It was full of Tibetans in very poor health due to their arduous journeys, the unfamiliar, scorchingly hot climate and the polluted water. Tuberculosis was rife. All the refugees became sick with between twenty and thirty people dying everyday, including Akong Rinpoche's elder brother Jamyang Chogyal. Akong Rinpoche also contracted TB sometime later but fortunately recovered as did his young brother, Jampal Drakpa who survived smallpox and tuberculosis, after a major operation to remove a lung.

Freda Bedi, who later became known as Sister Palmo after being ordained by His Holiness Karmapa, was deeply moved by the story of Akong Rinpoche and Trungpa Rinpoche. She thought they were in just about the worst state of any of the refugees she had encountered and she took a motherly interest in the two young Lamas. After a few months she began corresponding with Trungpa Rinpoche and eventually invited him to stay at her house in Delhi. Akong Rinpoche joined them soon after and the tulkus were treated like adopted sons by Mrs. Bedi who would work by day in the Civil Service and return home at night to look after her charges and teach them English. They in turn had a profound effect on her and it was due to their influence that she started the Tibetan Penfriendship Group in conjunction with a Mrs. Joyce Armstrong of the fledgling Buddhist Society in England. Another significant outcome of the tulku's time at Mrs. Bedi's home was the idea to establish the Young Lamas Home School in Dalhousie. As tulkus are reincarnate Lamas looked up to by other Tibetans it was especially important to educate them and pass on the Buddhas' teachings to that they in turn could guide others with wisdom and compassion.

Trungpa was appointed Principal of the school while Akong Rinpoche became Manager. The Rinpoches were well looked after and were in charge of teaching and taking care of other young tulkus in the Young Lamas Home School. Young Jampal Drakpa also joined them at the Home School in Dalhousie and was later sent to the study Administration and English at Buxadaur College to train for a job in the establishment of a new settlement for Tibetans in exile.

During the three years Akong Rinpoche and Trungpa Rinpoche spent under the aegis of Mrs. Bedi at the Young Lamas Home School they were taught English, often by an intrepid young English girl, Cherry Armstrong. Trungpa Rinpoche was particularly adept in the language and Mrs. Bedi managed to arrange for him to study comparative religion at Saint Anthony's College in Oxford. Although Akong Rinpoche's English was less fluent he was particularly interested in medicine. Indeed he was already a qualified Doctor of Tibetan Medicine and wanted to broaden his knowledge and gain some understanding of the western medical system. Consequently, Mrs. Bedi arrange a passage to England for the two Lamas.

The Lamas first travelled to His Holiness Karmapa's Monastery at Rumtek in Sikkim in order to take their leave and receive His Holiness's instructions and blessing before setting off on their historic journey to the unknown western world that awaited. Then after a two week voyage Akong Rinpoche and Trungpa Rinpoche disembarked on Thursday April 4th 1963 at Tilbury Dock where they were met by a welcoming party that included a Mr and Mrs Armstrong, the Venerable Ananda Bodhi and several members of the Buddhist Society. Joyce Armstrong was Secretary of the Tibetan Penfriendship Group in the UK and had been working closely with Freda Bedi in India. Indeed, it was Joyce's daughter Cherry who was at that time working with Freda Bedi in Dalhousie at the Young Lamas Home School where she had known the young Rinpoches and had spent many hours teaching them English.

Mrs. Armstrong remembers picking out the two burgundy robed figures in the crowd as they walked down the gangplank, followed by a large number of boxes, and greeted them as they first set foot on British soil. Once they had passed through customs the two young Tibetans were ushered into the Armstrong's Dormobile and driven to the Buddhist Society's base at Ovington Gardens. After being welcomed there and given a short rest they continued to the Armstrong's home in High Wycombe where they were to remain for the for the next few weeks while they acclimatised themselves. During that time they met many prominent British Buddhists, including the well known author Christmas Humphreys.

On moving to Oxford so that Trungpa Rinpoche could attend college they first stayed at Queen Elizabeth House Boarding College but their meagre budget was fast disappearing in paying the rent so the young Lamas tried to find cheaper accommodation in a family house. On hearing of their plight a Reverend John Larter wanted to help and told his wife that he would like to bring home two Lamas to stay. Mrs Larter thought he was talking about llamas and protested that their garden would not be big enough for such large creatures. However, once it was explained that the Lamas were people from Tibet and not animals from Peru she was quite agreeable to the idea and the Rinpoches spent several months in the Larter home.

Akong Rinpoche trained with the Red Cross, although his English was still rudimentary, nonetheless he managed to find work as a hospital orderly in Oxford's Churchill Hospital and was able to support himself and Trungpa Rinpoche with his wage. At first Akong Rinpoche found his menial work in the hospital "mental torture." In Tibet he had been enthroned as an Abbot and an incarnate Lama from the age of five and had always had people to do things for him. Suddenly he was in a strange country with the job of cleaning floors and toilets and wheeling patients around the hospital.

"If I hadn't had the Buddhist teachings and some understanding of the mind I would have hanged myself. It's quite hard being on a throne one day then cleaning toilets another," he mused, "but eventually I got to quite like my work and I'm now very grateful for the experience."

Akong Rinpoche's wage soon enabled him to find more independent accommodation for himself and Trungpa Rinpoche and after several moves they finally rented a modest basement flat in St. Margaret's Road. On visiting the Cambridge Buddhist Society they became friendly with a young man called Owen Matthews, who was later known as Lodro Thaye when he became the first person in the West to be ordained by Trungpa Rinpoche. Lodro Thaye moved in with the Lamas and meditated with them in the evenings then would go off to work in the Oxfordshire Constabulary by day. Before long they were joined by two more by friends, Lama Chime Rinpoche and the Master Artist Sherab Palden Beru, whom they had previously known at the Young Lamas Home School. All five lived in the same little flat, with only Akong Rinpoche working to support the Tibetans.

Dr. Bent Juel-Jensen, a staff physician at the hospital where Akong Rinpoche worked was impressed by the quiet, unassuming Tibetan and questioned him about his background. Having been posted to both Burma and India as a doctor in the army Dr. Juel Jensen knew something of the East and on learning that Akong Rinpoche was a High Lama and Doctor of Tibetan Medicine arranged a job for him at the Radcliffe Hospital working in the operating theatre where he could learn about western surgery and medical treatment. The work was much more interesting for Akong Rinpoche but there were long periods in between operations when he found himself unoccupied. Rinpoche took to collecting lengths of unused waste stitching thread from the operating theatre and taught himself to embroider. He became very skilled and someone gave him some coloured silk threads with which he made some very beautiful embroidered wall hangings of Tibetan mantras. Rinpoche then lent his newfound embroidery skills to repairing the kneelers in the local church, free of charge, "Because it was for the Church."

Chogyam Trungpa Rinpoche had also attracted attention, due in large part to the publication of his book 'Born in Tibet' which he had written in collaboration with an English woman, Esme Cramer Roberts. Before long Trungpa Rinpoche began giving meditation classes in their cramped flat to a growing number of Oxford academics and members of the Oxford Buddhist Society, amongst whom was its Secretary John Maxwell, a young law student who later became a long term friend. When the BBC got wind of the Tibetan Lama's presence and made a programme about them even more meditation students started to turn up. It soon became clear that they would need to relocate to bigger premises. A cutting from The Guardian dated the fourth of April 1964 spoke of the two refugee Lamas hoping "to set up a study Centre in Oxford".

The Armstrong family were instrumental in searching for alternative accommodation where the tulkus could establish a Tibetan Centre and had looked at various properties, not only around Oxford but as far a field as Cornwall and Yorkshire. Meanwhile their own house in High Wycombe was always open to the Tibetan Lamas who continued to visit on numerous occasions, including that of Cherry Armstrong's marriage to Luke Hindmarsh, which was the first Tibetan Buddhist wedding blessing to be conducted in England. Eventually, in early 1967 their search led them to a former hunting lodge set in spacious grounds situated in the tranquil, unspoilt countryside of the Scottish borders.

Chogyam Trungpa Rinpoche, Sister Palmo and Akong Tulku Rinpoche in India

The Rinpoches with Prime Minister Nehru

At the Young Lamas School

*Chogyam Trungpa Rinpoche and
Akong Tulku Rinpoche in India*

The Rinpoches at High Wycombe

The Rinpoches at Oxford

CHAPTER 2

TAKING ROOT

Johnstone House stands in a lush green valley where the river Esk winds its way through the grounds, past rolling hills studded with grazing sheep and cattle. In 1963 the property was owned by the Johnstone House Trust which was founded by a western ordained Buddhist monk, the Venerable Ananda Bodhi, as a broad based religious community dedicated to fostering human understanding. The community had a strong affinity with the Buddhist philosophy and on several occasions invited the young Tibetan Lamas living in Oxford to come and give teachings. However, just as the Johnstone House community's funding and administrative difficulties caused it to decline so interest in the Tibetan Buddhist Lamas was gaining momentum. The Trustees therefore considered selling the property to the Tibetans and their followers.

Although the Lamas had already given teachings at Johnstone House they had not really looked at it from the point of view of prospective buyers. Accordingly, even though they did not actually have funds to purchase it, they decided to view it with that in mind. As Akong Rinpoche was busy working at the hospital Trungpa Rinpoche and artist, Sherab Palden arranged to go and look the place over. Although it was a substantial property in extensive grounds the house itself was not in the best state of repair, being rather cold and damp, and would be difficult to refurbish and maintain. Trungpa Rinpoche and Sherab Palden telephoned Akong Rinpoche in Oxford and told him as much. However, Akong Rinpoche was in no doubt and said they should get it. Quite how that was to be accomplished without funds seemed not to be an issue.

As the Johnstone Trust had been set up to relieve suffering and make the Buddhist teachings available, it was clearly in line with the aspirations of the Tibetans. Consequently, one of the Trustees, a Mr. Robert Copley, came up with a brilliant idea to circumvent the Tibetan's lack of finance. He suggested that the Tibetans take over administration of the Trust by themselves becoming Trustees. The idea was taken up by the other Trustees and so it was that on March 19th 1967, without any money changing hands, the two young Lamas found themselves co-founders of what was to become the first Tibetan Buddhist Centre in the West.

Akong Rinpoche went back to Oxford to finish his work at the hospital while Trungpa Rinpoche and Sherab Palden installed themselves in their new home set in the vast open spaces of the Scottish countryside, so reminiscent of their Tibetan homeland. Several months later, during the summer of '67, Akong Rinpoche said goodbye to Oxford's dreaming spires and boarded a bus bound for Lockerbie. On arrival he was met by one of the young western residents of Johnstone House who had been sent to collect him. The half hour drive from Lockerbie to Eskdalemuir was pleasant and uneventful until the car they were travelling in reached Eskdalemuir Village Church where it shuddered to a halt and refused to budge. Rinpoche simply got out and completed the last mile of his journey on foot, enjoying the scenery and fresh country air as he strolled along the road to his new home. Once installed at Johnstone House, Akong Rinpoche and a handful of volunteers set about repairing and refurbishing the place. The lack of available funds severely curtailed these efforts but the goodwill and pioneering spirit nevertheless contrived to make the place habitable. Meanwhile Trungpa Rinpoche gave some basic teachings, both at Johnstone House and in various schools and halls.

At first Akong Rinpoche and Trungpa Rinpoche thought about calling their new residence the Tibetan Monastic Centre, but then realised that was too narrow a title that sounded as if it was a place only for monks. They then decided to call it Samye Ling after the great Samye Monastery in Tibet, which was founded in the 8th Century by Guru Rinpoche, also known as Padmasambhava, or the second Buddha. It was the Himalayan kingdom's first Buddhist Monastery and Cultural Centre through which the entire Buddhist canon had been transplanted from India to Tibet. It was hoped that the Scottish based Samye Ling, which means 'place beyond concept', would follow in the example of its illustrious predecessor and bring the precious teachings of Buddha to the West.

The summer of '67 in the UK, sometimes referred to as the summer of love, was the height of hippy culture, a time of breaking through class and social barriers, of experimentation and searching for alternative life styles, of rejecting war and materialism in favour of peace and idealism. Western youth was disillusioned with the capitalist values of their elders and in seeking a more spiritual path many of them turned their eyes eastwards. Some made quests to India, Nepal, Bali and Thailand, whilst others found their search led them to the rather more domestic destination of Eskdalemuir in the borders of Scotland. With the arrival of the young Tibetan Buddhist Lamas, the East had come west.

One of the first people to find their way to Samye Ling was Harry Milward who, at the time of writing, is a sprightly ninety five year old Samye Ling resident happily ensconced in his riverside timber frame house. As a young man in the army Harry had been posted to India where he was exposed to eastern culture and religions. On leaving the army he was based in London where he worked as an engineer for the Plessy Group. He was also an active member of the Gurdjieff Society, part of whose remit was to study all the world religions. Harry chose to explore Buddhism and soon found that there was very little writing on the subject and almost nothing on Tibetan Buddhism. Having heard about the recent opening of Samye Ling on the Gurdjieff Society grapevine, Harry drove up to Scotland in the autumn of '67 determined to find out what he could about this mysterious religion.

Recalling his visit to Samye Ling, Harry shakes with laughter at the memory of his first impressions. "I opened the door of this old fashioned Scottish hunting lodge to find it full of hippy types with long hair and flowing clothes. As I was a fifty one year old business executive and engineer I felt rather like a fish out of water. Nevertheless I made some enquiries and was told I could make an appointment with Trungpa Rinopoche for the following day."

Harry then explored the grounds and noticed the beginnings of a garden, an outhouse serving as a pottery, and a barn full of junk. The house itself he thought rather threadbare and the shared bedrooms somewhat Spartan, cold and damp. After an edible but not particularly appetising lunch of rice and lentils he elected to stay in a bed and breakfast in Eskdalemuir village and return for his appointment the next day.

Chogyam Trungpa Rinpoche had chosen one of the bay windowed front rooms of Johnstone House for his office and it was there that Harry Millward first set eyes on the confident young Lama. After shaking hands the two men sat down to talk. On hearing Trungpa Rinpoche's excellent command of English, with his newly acquired Oxford veneer, Harry felt able to pose numerous questions regarding Tibetan Buddhism. Trungpa Rinpoche answered clearly, recommended further reading, and generally impressed his interlocutor with his knowledge and charisma. When they fell to talking about Gurdjieff it was clear that Trungpa Rinpoche was acquainted with his philosophy as he pointed out that, "What the Gurdjieff people call 'self remembering' is, at its best, what Buddhists would term 'mindfulness'."

Harry felt he had been given much food for thought and accordingly he went away to think on and digest all his newly acquired information. After a few days he came back for a second helping and was further impressed by Trungpa Rinpoche's direct manner and genuine erudition. Nonetheless, Harry came away feeling that although Buddhism was evidently a good and true religion it was perhaps better suited to people from the East rather than to Westerners who might not understand.

As he wandered round the grounds of Samye Ling Harry bumped into another Tibetan in monk's robes who appeared to be about the same age as Trungpa Rinpoche. They fell into conversation and the young monk introduced himself simply as Akong. Harry had no idea that Akong was also a reincarnate Lama as they chatted first about Gurdjieff and then about more practical matters. Harry mentioned that he'd noticed how cold and damp the bedrooms were in Johnstone House and found himself volunteering to put his engineering skills at Samye Ling's disposal by improving and extending the heating system. Akong Rinpoche gladly accepted the offer and Harry agreed to take time off work and return the following spring.

After what must have been a cold and uncomfortable first winter in Scotland for the Tibetans Harry was as good as his word and returned to Samye Ling in the spring of '68. Trungpa Rinpoche was away at the time but Akong Rinpoche was managing the Centre and walked round with Harry as he surveyed the ancient and inadequate boiler room and heating system. A list was made of all the parts needed to improve it and Harry agreed to come back again and do the work for free provided the parts were bought and he could have some assistants. This was agreed on and accordingly Harry returned once again in August.

On Harry's third visit to Samye Ling Trungpa Rinpoche was away once more, visiting the US. However, Harry felt himself drawn to the modest young monk with the calm air of self possession that he still knew simply as Akong. Their communications tended to be about practical matters and as Akong Rinpoche had managed to purchase all the necessary parts and provide assistants Harry was able to get on with his work to improve the heating. Once that was accomplished he instructed Akong Rinpoche in its use and said it would have to be switched on for at least two or three hours a day in order to heat the building. Akong Rinpoche replied that they couldn't afford to do that and that one hour a day would have to do. Harry then insisted that one hour a day would be virtually useless and that two hours would be the bare minimum, at which point Akong Rinpoche merely smiled and nodded, but Harry had the distinct impression that his words had fallen on deaf ears.

The resident community at that time numbered only a dozen or so people, most of whom were sleeping in shared rooms. Life was still quite tough, especially in the winter. Nevertheless there was a growing sense of community and people put up with the Spartan living conditions in order to experience a greater sense of meaning in their lives. Akong Rinpoche did what he could to improve things, despite the lack of funds, and from time to time donations of various goods and equipment would come in so that gradually the Centre was able to accommodate more people, albeit in a rather rough and ready way. One such person was Mamie Bannerman, a young Scottish woman who, after spending time in India, enrolled at a college in Glasgow to study Social Work. On hearing about the Tibetan Lamas from a college friend, Mamie sent a letter addressed to The Tibetans, Dumfriesshire asking if she could come. Amazingly she received a note a week later from Akong Rinpoche telling her to "come and see us".

The following weekend Mamie hitchhiked down to Eskdalemuir and booked in at Samye Ling. Her room in Johnstone House was shared with several other people. Sleeping on a mattress on the floor Mamie spent her first night dozing fitfully to the sound of the rats scrabbling about in the rafters. Nevertheless she was drawn to the Tibetans who seemed so calm and accepting of everyone and everything. She remembers Trungpa Rinpoche chiefly teaching meditation, Sherab Palden painting thangkas and Akong Rinpoche doing all the household work nobody else would do.

" I felt sorry for Akong Rinpoche," said Mamie, "he was always working so hard and although he made a cleaning rota nobody seemed to take much notice. They were all too busy looking for enlightenment."

Mamie decided to offer her help and would often hitchhike to Samye Ling, sometimes with her two young children in tow, to spend the weekends helping Akong Rinpoche with the chores. On one occasion they spent an entire weekend mending old sheets that had been donated to the Centre. As they worked together, cutting out the worn parts of the sheets then sewing the good parts together, Mamie developed great respect for the young Lama who taught by his example. Some time later she presented Akong Rinpoche with a white silk katta, or ceremonial scarf, and took Refuge with him, as did her daughter Chaya and son Kumar in their own time.

Trungpa Rinpoche meanwhile continued to give teachings both at Samye Ling and in other Buddhist oriented places in the UK. One such place, also founded by Ananda Bodhi, was a Theravadin Centre in Staffordshire called Old Biddulph Hall where Trungpa Rinpoche had been invited to give a course in meditation. The people enrolled on the course had never come into contact with Tibetan Buddhism before and were intrigued by the young Lama's light and humorous approach. One young woman, Carol Sagar, described him as, "a shiny, light being, very receptive, sensitive and playful." As her health had been problematic Carol divided her time at Biddulph between meditation sessions, resting and painting. When Trungpa Rinpoche discovered Carol was ill and that she painted he would go to her room everyday, sit on the floor and paint with her. Their point of contact was through the painting but they would talk of many things and in this informal way Trungpa Rinpoche taught her through all his activities. He also recommended that she should go to Samye Ling to see Akong Rinpoche who was a Doctor of Tibetan Medicine and would be able to help her back to health.

Akong Rinpoche meanwhile was busy trying to make Samye Ling a worthy repository for the Buddhist teachings. The largest of the downstairs rooms, which had formerly been a trophy room in the old hunting lodge, had been transformed into a beautiful shrine room. It had been painted in glowing colours and was adorned with traditional thangkas painted by Sherab Palden. Well ensconced in Samye Ling, Sherab was working away to produce masterpieces of Tibetan Art, not only for Samye Ling but for various other Centres and Buddhist art collectors around the world, his reputation as a Master of the Karma Gadri School having been further enhanced by exhibitions of his work in London. Akong Rinpoche and Trungpa Rinpoche would take turns to return to India to see his Holiness the 16th Gyalwa Karmapa and seek his advice on how to proceed with the new Centre which, being the first such place of its kind, was in the vanguard of bringing the precious Tibetan Buddhist teachings to the West. On one such trip Trungpa Rinpoche met up with Akong Rinpoche's younger brother, Jampal Drakpa, known as Jamdrak for short.

When Akong Rinpoche and Trungpa Rinpoche had left India for the UK in 1963 young Jamdrak had stayed to complete his education and had subsequently worked for a time helping to establish a permanent settlement for Tibetan refugees. However, on meeting His Holiness the Karmapa in New Delhi in 1967 he was offered the chance to go and stay at the Karmapa's Rumtek Monastery in Sikkim. Jamdrak felt such a connection to the head of the Kagyu Lineage that he had no hesitation in leaving his well paid job to join the Karmapa at Rumtek. He was given the responsible position of Private Secretary and travelled to Bhutan and other places with His Holiness.

At Rumtek Jamdrak was given his own room alongside the four young Kagyu heart sons, namely Khentin Tai Situpa, Kunzik Sharmapa, Goshir Gyaltsapa and Jamgon Kongtrul Rinpoche. While the Rinpoches were studying Jamdrak would practice the Four Foundations and was given the rare privilege of doing his practice in the inner sanctum of the relics room which contained holy relics of all the previous Karmapas. Although Jamdrak was a lay person he nevertheless found himself in the privileged position of living alongside these young High Lamas and of receiving teachings from the highest teachers of the Kagyu Lineage. It was a great honour but one for which the young Jamdrak was not entirely ready.

Whilst in Sikkim Jamdrak had come into contact with some young Americans who were working for the Peace Corps. He liked the casual way they dressed and was fascinated by their free and easy lifestyle. Wanting to experience more of Western culture Jamdrak asked His Holiness if he could go to the UK to join his brother Akong Rinpoche and Trungpa Rinpoche at Samye Ling. His Holiness did not think it was a good idea and refused his permission.

Some time later, when His Holiness was away Jamdrak heard that Trungpa Rinpoche was in India. He lost no time in travelling to New Delhi to meet up with his old friend and enlist his help. Jamdrak accompanied Trungpa Rinpoche to the Canadian High Commission and, through their combined charm offensive and string pulling, a passport and visa that could often take years to process, was duly obtained within two months.

It was 1969 when Jamdrak arrived in the UK after an adventurous trip in the company of his friend and mentor Trungpa Rinpoche, who readily introduced his young countryman to the weird and wonderful ways of sixties western culture. Jamdrak threw himself headlong into the hippy hedonism of that time. His more sober brother Akong Rinpoche had been used to shouldering responsibilities from an early age and was not so fascinated by the ephemeral whims and fashions of the day. He tried to be both a mother and father to Jamdrak and indulged his wishes, doing his best to give him whatever he asked for. On one occasion, when Akong Rinpoche left for India to visit His Holiness Karmapa, he entrusted Jamdrak with the day to day running of Samye Ling.

At that time Jamdrak was not interested in the spiritual life. He didn't even go inside the shrine room. But he was good at organisation and administration and managed to keep the Centre running in his brother's absence, although there was a definite sense of 'while the cat's away the mice will play' during that time. Indeed it was then that Trungpa Rinpoche decided to buy a car. His driving skills were questionable and one day when driving to Newcastle he crashed the car through the wall of a joke shop. The accident though was no laughing matter and left Trungpa Rinpoche severely paralysed in hospital for several months. Jamdrak and Sherab Palden made frequent visits to the hospital where Trungpa lay unable to move. Very gradually he started to recover and Sherab Palden recalls his first hand movements were a series of mudras, (symbolic hand movements used in Buddhist prayers).

When Akong Rinpoche returned from India he was shocked to find his friend in such a state. As soon as Trungpa Rinpoche was well enough to leave hospital he went to stay with one of his students who lived not far from Samye Ling in a place called Garwald. Situated up a farm track a mile and a half away from Samye Ling, Garwald provided a more secluded and peaceful environment in which Trungpa Rinpoche could recuperate. It was a slow and painstaking process but Trungpa Rinpoche gradually recovered the use of his limbs and eventually started to walk again.

It was during his convalescence that Trungpa Rinpoche decided to give up his monk's robes and become a lay person. His charismatic presence and increasingly unconventional behaviour mystified some people and attracted others. One person who was definitely attracted was a young woman called Diane Pybus. The feeling was evidently mutual for the couple decided to get married on the 4th of January 1970. A year later Trungpa Rinpoche elected to leave Scotland and make a home with his young wife in the US. He had already visited the States at the request of some American students and felt that his style of teaching would be better suited to the American psyche. Consequently he left Samye Ling in 1971 and travelled to the US where he would eventually set up several influential Dharma Centres and write some of the most compelling books on Tibetan Buddhism ever to appear in the English Language.

The Venerable Ananda Bodhi (centre) with residents and guest at Johnstone House

Sherab Palden Beru, Trungpa Rinpoche and Akong Rinpoche at Johnstone House

Akong Rinpoche sewing

CHAPTER III

NOURISHMENT

With Trungpa Rinpoche's departure Akong Rinpoche was thrust onto centre stage at Samye Ling, a position that he felt reluctant to occupy. He had always been content to let Trungpa Rinpoche do the teaching while he concerned himself with the practicalities of setting up and running the Centre. Although his command of English was in no way as sophisticated as Trungpa Rinpoche's, nonetheless Akong Rinpoche communicated on a deep and subtle level with those around him. The cloak of his humble and unassuming presence began to open and reveal something of the profound depths of his wisdom and compassion, coupled with an immense strength and integrity that belied his still tender years.

Having sought the advice of His Holiness Karmapa, Akong Rinpoche had been encouraged to give teachings at Samye Ling and had also been promised the support of His Holiness and all the other High Lamas of the Kagyu Lineage. With the blessings of His Holiness as his support and inspiration Akong Rinpoche purposefully took up the reins to steer Samye Ling on a wise and steady course of progress to become a spiritual oasis and a place of refuge for people seeking a deeper sense of meaning in their lives. His training as a Doctor of Tibetan Medicine and skill as a healer informed his approach from the beginning and made Samye Ling as much a place of therapy and healing as a centre for Buddhist teachings and meditation. Akong Rinpoche made himself accessible to all comers and would help them in whichever way was most appropriate to their needs. Feeling that his exotic monks robes set him apart somewhat from the people he decided to dress in lay clothes and blend in more with the locals. He would sit with the resident community at morning meditation, eat his meals and work with them throughout the day, then attend the evening prayers in what felt like a family atmosphere.

Akong Rinpoche had by this time also started his own family. Having met Yangchen, a young Tibetan woman, the couple duly got married in 1971, with their good friend Chime Rinpoche acting as best man. Thanks to the generous support of several kind benefactors who had known Akong Rinpoche when he was still in Oxford, the young couple were able to set up house in Dumfries. Yangchen ran the house as a Bed and Breakfast place and at weekends Rinpoche would join her and help with the chores. The B and B enabled Rinpoche to be financially independent. Then as now Samye Ling was always run entirely by volunteers and Akong Rinpoche has always been scrupulous over the years in keeping any income and donations to the Centre entirely separate from his personal family finances.

Visitors to the Centre were often surprised at Akong Rinpoche's modest and down to earth demeanour. Never afraid of getting his hands dirty Rinpoche would often be found cleaning out a drain or shovelling rubble and had sometimes been mistaken for a labourer rather than the head of the first Kagyu Buddhist Centre in the West. On getting to know him better, people became drawn as to a magnet by the sheer power of his compassion and loving kindness. One such person was Carol Sagar, the young woman who had previously met Trungpa Rinpoche in 1967 when he had advised her to see Akong Rinpoche about her ailing health. However, it was not until 1971 that Carol finally came to follow that advice and make the journey from her home in Hertfordshire to the borders of Scotland.

Carol had been extremely ill in hospital with respiratory problems, but as soon as she felt well enough she decided to seek out Akong Rinpoche. On arrival at Samye Ling Carol made an appointment and was soon shown in to the front room office. She found Akong Rinpoche, wearing ordinary lay clothes, sitting on a cushion on the floor. He beckoned her to sit down on another cushion and Carol felt an immediate sense of trust in the young Lama who gave off an air of calm and gentleness. She told him of her illness and after a few moments Akong Rinpoche simply said, "I think I can help you". Carol felt an immediate sense of relief and confidence in him, "and boy did he ever help me!" she enthuses, "and he's been helping me ever since".

From the outset Akong Rinpoche preferred to teach people on a one to one basis according to their different needs, rather than give public teachings. However, he did invite the very best Buddhist teachers to lead courses at Samye Ling. In order to do so he first had to be able to offer decent accommodation for the visiting teachers, High Lamas and attendant monks. The first major step towards this was the conversion of the old barns adjacent to Johnstone House into a new accommodation block. On completion of the building, community members worked on the interior decoration, under the direction of Sherab Palden and several beautiful murals were painted to adorn the hall and stairway. This additional housing block was referred to as 'the New Building' for many years but since other new buildings have gone up it is now known as Tashi Deleg House.

Akong Rinpoche put great effort into ensuring that all the teachings at Samye Ling were of an impeccable standard and given by the highest masters of their particular tradition. Initially there were teachings by monks from Thailand, Burma and Japan who gave courses from the Theravadin and Zen traditions. Gradually, as more Lamas arrived from Tibet and India there was a shift to the Mahayana and Vajrayana teachings of Tibetan Buddhism. A full list of these teachings, from 1972 until the present day, is available in Chapter XVII where they are listed in chronological order. Many of them are also available on tape and form part of a priceless heritage of Buddhist wisdom handed down from great masters to western students for the benefit of all beings.

The visits of these illustrious teachers created a unique opportunity which drew people from many parts of the world to study and receive teachings and empowerments from the very pinnacle of Tibetan Buddhist masters. Consequently, awareness of Samye Ling grew both nationally and internationally as the Centre established a reputation of excellence and authenticity. Such revered beings as His Holiness the 16th Gyalwa Karmapa, the very Venerable Kalu Rinpoche and many others visited for the first time in early nineteen seventies. Kalu Rinpoche first came in 1972 then again in '74 and 75 accompanied by many other experienced Lamas. This enabled the full performance of Tibetan Buddhist prayers, empowerments and ceremonies, with the sacred music of traditional Tibetan instruments such as the jahling and rhadong, to echo through the Scottish hills and valleys for the very first time.

Another major milestone in Samye Ling's history was the first visit of the head of the Kagyu Lineage, His Holiness the 16th Gyalwa Karmapa in 1974. Before coming to Scotland His Holiness was scheduled to travel to the United States. Akong Rinpoche went to meet His Holiness at London airport during his stop over before his plane proceeded to the States.

Rinpoche hired a suite of rooms for His Holiness and the entourage so that they could be comfortable while details of His Holiness's visit to the UK were discussed and finalised. On Rinpoche's return to Samye Ling preparations for the visit began. Lama Orgyen, Sherab Palden and John Chinnery all co-operated in the making of a fine throne while many visitors worked alongside the residents, often late into the night, cleaning and decorating the house, re-arranging the shrine room, and generally making the place as comfortable as possible to receive their revered guest and his party.

On November 12th 1974, after a highly successful tour of many new Centres in North America, His Holiness flew into Prestwick airport accompanied by twelve Lamas. Several cars were sent from Samye Ling to bring His Holiness' party to the Centre. On arrival His Holiness went straight to the shrine room to pray and give blessings. The following day was New Moon Day, which is considered an auspicious time for accomplishing religious ceremonies. His Holiness performed the Black Crown ceremony for the benefit of all beings. This sacred rite, performed exclusively by the lineage of the Karmapas, bestows tremendous blessings on all those who are fortunate enough to witness it. The shrine room was filled to bursting with people and many others lined the corridors outside. His Holiness gave blessings to every single person present and also gave the Milarepa Empowerment, thus enabling Buddhist students to practice the Guru Yoga of the holy saint and yogi Milarepa.

His Holiness spent several weeks in the UK and was based at Samye Ling throughout his visit. His party of twelve Lamas and monks included Tulku Tenga Rinpoche who acted as Dorje Loppon, or prayer master, and also gave Dharma teachings. Another member of the party was Akong Rinpoche's dear friend from the Young Lamas Home School in Dalhousie, Freda Bedi. Having since taken ordination with His Holiness Karmapa she was now known as the Venerable Sister Palmo. As a seasoned western Buddhist practitioner Sister Palmo was very helpful in giving much practical advice to the budding Buddhist community. During this historic visit His Holiness gave Refuge, Bodhisattva Vows, teachings and ceremonies for many people at Samye Ling as well as in Edinburgh, Birmingham, Cambridge and London, thus setting them on the Buddhist Path. While at Samye Ling, His Holiness also bestowed many precious empowerments, namely the previously mentioned empowerment of Milarepa and subsequently those of Karma Pakshi, Sangye Menla, Manjushri and Chenrezig.

During the third week of his visit, on the auspicious occasion of the Full Moon Day, His Holiness gave the first full Buddhist ordinations ever held in Europe when he ordained ten Western practitioners. On the evening of that same day he bestowed the last Vajra Crown Ceremony of his visit followed by a Chenrezig initiation. This precious time during His Holiness' stay made a tremendous impact on everyone who was fortunate enough to meet him and be touched by his radiant presence.

As well as the visit of His Holiness Karmapa, who was head of the Kagyu Lineage, Samye Ling also hosted in the ensuing years, visits from great teachers of all the main Tibetan Buddhist Lineages, namely His Holiness the Dalai Lama, Dilgo Khyentse Rinpoche and Sakya Tenzin Rinpoche amongst others. The presence of such realised beings had a profound affect on residents and visitors alike, resulting in many more people being drawn to stay and become part of the community at Samye Ling, with each of them bringing their various skills, crafts, and labour to help the Centre grow.

Accommodation was still at a premium, but gradually some wooden huts sprang up near the river and several workshop spaces were created to house different activities. A small shop was opened selling the basic essentials required for community life from Buddhist texts to toothpaste. Samye Ling was starting to flourish. The Centre even ran its own farm with a small herd of dairy cattle providing milk, butter, yoghurt and cheese. Later, in the mid 80's, the farm was extended to include worker's accommodation, a cow byre and a large barn built nearby the river to the rear of the neighbouring property of Old Johnstone. A herd of up to twenty cows was looked after by a succession of farm hands, notably Paul and Betty Richardson then Jan Lageweg and more recently Paul Gilbert, with some of the main dairy workers being Elise Jacobsen, Jane Good and Aldo.

Much of Samye Ling's land was designated as gardens and in the early years the lawns and flower gardens in front of Johnstone house were lovingly tended and cultivated by Elizabeth McIntyre who planted a wide range of flowers and shrubs, many of which originated in Tibet. A small lake, which Ron Long originally dug out by hand, with the help of an old army Jeep, was extended some years later and stocked with fish and water plants. At its centre a miniature island with a stone Buddha shrine could be reached by way of a picturesque wooden bridge providing a tranquil and delightful little haven for both humans and waterfowl.

Vegetable gardens were also an important part of community life and the early plots first started by John and Nancy Chinnery were further developed by Bernard Provost then extended and currently looked after by head gardener Tony Freck and an enthusiastic team of assistants. As well as supplying the Centre with organic herbs and vegetables the gardens have also provided many people with a wholesome and therapeutic working environment where they have been able to their renew their connection to nature. It was not uncommon for Akong Rinpoche to prescribe a spell of gardening to alleviate troubled minds.

Meanwhile, Akong Rinpoche's young brother Jamdrak was living in a parallel universe. He rarely came to Samye Ling, preferring to make his base at Rinpoche's family home in Dumfries from where he continued his relentless pursuit of pleasure. Having acquired a boutique, a motorbike then a car Jamdrak immersed himself in western lifestyle with a vengeance, spending his time smoking, drinking and partying with new found friends yet never really feeling any satisfaction. The turning point came when Jamdrak was asked to accompany a family friend on a fishing trip to the Orkneys.

Although Jamdrak wasn't really happy with the idea of fishing, as it went against his Buddhist upbringing, he didn't want to disappoint his friend David Robertson, so he agreed to go. Even though he had never fished before it seems the fish just found his hook and by the end of the day he had landed a large heap of fish. Jamdrak couldn't actually bring himself to kill the fish so his friend obliged by hitting them over the head. David was so pleased with their catch that he took photographs of Jamdrak standing beside the pile of dead fish and on their return to Dumfries he proudly showed Akong Rinpoche the pictures.

For the first time in Jamdrak's life he saw his elder brother become visibly moved. As Akong Rinpoche took him to one side to speak to him man to man his face looked so sad. He explained to Jamdrak that he had promised their parents that he would look after him. He had done his best to be both father and mother to Jamdrak and to give him everything he had asked for. Rinpoche explained that he had tried to bring him up as a decent person and a good Buddhist but now he felt he had failed and he could not be at peace with their parents.

These words wrenched Jamdrak's heart. Before that moment he had somewhat resented his brother and held him responsible for the fact that he had been separated from their parents at a young age when he had to leave home to go to Akong Rinpoche's monastery. Suddenly he saw how wrong he had been and how selfishly he had acted. He realized how kind Akong Rinpoche had been to him, always sacrificing his own needs to give him everything he wanted.

"If he had beaten me it could not have been worse than the pain I felt at his words. Really his kindness could have changed the heart of a monster. From that moment on I was no longer interested in rebelling and fighting against him. I decided there and then to do something to make him happy and proud of me."

Shortly after this dramatic change of heart Jamdrak heard that His Holiness Karmapa was touring in the United States. Having run away from His Holiness's Monastery in Sikkim before embarking on his time of rebellion in the West, Jamdrak knew he had to seek His Holiness's forgiveness and blessing in order to truly turn over a new leaf and get his life back on track. He begged Akong Rinpoche to let him go to America and join His Holiness. Rinpoche was only too pleased to accede to this request and so it was that Jamdrak found himself in the US being welcomed back by His Holiness like a prodigal son returning to his forgiving and compassionate father.

Jamdrak travelled extensively in the US with His Holiness and the fifteen other monks in his party. Whilst visiting Niagara Falls His Holiness took Jamdrak and a young monk called Karma Tenzin to one side. He explained to them that he had been offered a sum of money by a wealthy benefactor in order to start a Dharma Centre in New York and that he wanted Jamdrak and Tenzin to set it up. The young men were dumbfounded at this request since neither of them had any previous experience with such a project and could barely look after themselves let alone anyone else. However, their devotion to His Holiness made it impossible for them to refuse and, much to their own surprise they found themselves agreeing to carry out His Holiness's wishes.

Within a short time Jamdrak and Tenzin started a small Centre in New York. They invited several eminent Tibetan Lamas to teach there, including Khenpo Karthar, Bardor Tulku Rinpoche and Lama Ganga. The young men's hard work and diligence impressed their benefactor and before long they were offered a substantial property with land in New York State near the small town of Woodstock, which became the new Centre now known as Karma Triyana Dharmachakra. In brief, once Jamdrak had seen the error of his ways and had become disillusioned with pursuing a solely materialistic lifestyle he put his considerable energies to a more meaningful purpose and became the successful co-manager and treasurer of what is now the main seat of His Holiness Karmapa in the United States.

It was as a direct consequence of His Holiness's first visit to the West that his Dharma activity began to be felt around the world. While Jamdrak was busy establishing the new Centre in New York, Akong Rinpoche was presiding over a Samye Ling that was no longer seen by some as an exotic hangout for a few way out hippies, but rather as a fully fledged Centre of Tibetan Buddhism and Culture with a precious legacy of spiritual and cultural wealth to offer the world. Having been nourished by the teachings and blessings of His Holiness Karmapa and many other illustrious Masters, Samye Ling was coming of age.

Akong Rinpoche teaching in the shrine room

His Holiness The 16th Gyalwa Karmapa performing the Vajra Crown Cermony

Kalu Rinpoche at Samye Ling

Khenpo Tsultrim Gyamtso

32

His Emminence Goshir Gyaltsapa

Dilgo Khyentse Rinpoche

H.H. Sakya Tenzin Rinpoche

Akong Rinpoche and Jamdrak

Betty Richardson down on the farm

Sister Palmo at Samye Ling

CHAPTER IV

GROWTH

Many members of the Samye Ling community had developed a genuine wish to further their knowledge and practice of Buddhism. They had often asked Akong Rinpoche to give public teachings but had always received a negative response. Rinpoche taught people on an individual basis but preferred to leave public teachings to the many eminent teachers he invited. However, when the Karmapa was staying at Samye Ling the Buddhist residents asked His Holiness if he could persuade Akong Rinpoche to teach. On receiving this command from the head of the Kagyu Lineage Akong Rinpoche could hardly refuse and from 1975 onwards he finally agreed to give one or two courses a year.

Then, as now, Akong Rinpoche was not given to lengthy explanations or intellectual pyrotechnics, but his simple mode of expression seemed to strike at the very heart of his listeners and impart a real sense of the core of Buddhist teachings. In 1975 Akong Rinpoche gave his first public teaching on The Four Ways of Changing the Mind. That was followed by Teachings on the Four Preliminary Practices, then an Introduction to Guru Yoga, followed by a five week course on Guru Yoga which became something of a seminal milestone in the lives of many of the participants. Perhaps the most instructive aspect of all Rinpoche's teachings over the years lay in the faultless example of his application of Boddhicitta in daily life, his unfailing kindness and his total dedication to helping others according to their needs.

From the outset Akong Rinpoche had established Samye Ling as a place of protection and shelter for anyone who needed help, be it spiritual, charitable or therapeutic. In the years to come all these different aspects of his work developed into seperate multinational projects under the umbrella of the Rokpa Trust but in the early days people of all faiths and backgrounds would be drawn to Samye Ling, seeking not only Buddhist teachings and meditation advice but also help with a multitude of personal problems. Many such seekers came from overseas and as a result of receiving help and teachings at Samye Ling returned home to set up satellite Centres under the spiritual direction of Aking Rinpoche. Some of the first such Centres, or Samye Dzongs, were established in Belgium, Ireland, South Africa and Spain. Details of these can be found in Chapter XVII.

Regarding the practical work of running Samye Ling, Akong Rinpoche was greatly helped by the arrival of Ani Yeshe Zangmo, a friend of Sister Palmo, who arrived in the early seventies at the suggestion of His Holiness Karmapa. Ani Yeshe was the first ordained western resident at Samye Ling, having first taken novice ordination with his Holiness then in later years taking full ordination in Hong Kong. In addition to her sincere interest in the Dharma her previous experience as a business woman made her ideally placed to serve as Akong Rinpoche's secretary and also help with the day to day running of the Centre. This included making arrangements for the visits of many High Lamas.

In 1977 Akong Rinpoche invited His Holiness Karmapa once again to Samye Ling and indeed organised his entire six month trip around Europe to the many other Dharma Centres that had started to spring up in Samye Ling's wake. This second visit was a major undertaking, not only for Akong Rinpoche but for the community as a whole who worked for many months in preparation for the visit. It was winter when His Holiness arrived, accompanied by many High Lamas and monks, amongst who was one of the four Kagyu Heart Sons, Jamgon Kongtrul Rinpoche and the renowned yogi scholar Khenpo Tsultrim Gyamtso, both of whom gave teachings never before heard at Samye Ling.

As on the occasion of his first visit His Holiness gave the Refuge Ceremony enabling many more people to enter the Buddhist faith. However, the second time round there were far too many people to fit into Samye Ling's small shrine room so His Holiness performed the ceremony in the local Eskdalemuir Village Hall. Amongst those taking Refuge was Akong Rinpoche's present personal assistant, Ani Tsultrim Zangmo. Her recollection is of a blissful time in the radiant presence of His Holiness alongside the other people taking Refuge, including some twenty five or so children. Although the ceremony was held in the depths of winter on Christmas day, the heat of so many people crammed inside the village hall caused clouds of butterflies to emerge as if by magic. His Holiness also performed the Black Crown Ceremony in the same venue, which Ani Tsultrim recalls as being a time of great blessing. It was dark by the time everyone left the hall and as they came outside they noticed a beautiful many coloured rainbow encircling the moon. Groups of happy people walked backwards to Samye Ling while staring entranced at the miraculous apparition in the night sky.

Harry Milward and his wife Gwen had also come to Samye Ling to see His Holiness. Indeed Harry, who had previously improved and extended the heating system in Johnstone House had also put his engineering skills at Samye Ling's disposal, in preparation for Karmapa's visit by replacing all the old lead heating pipes, an extensive operation which required digging trenches up an adjacent hill. During his stay His Holiness wished to visit the nearby town of Lockerbie. As Harry owned the most respectable car on the premises he was given the welcome job of driving His Holiness into town. After rushing around cleaning and polishing his vehicle Harry sat inside expectantly waiting for His Holiness.

The first person to arrive was the young Jamgon Kongtrul who climbed in and started chatting amiably. However, before His Holiness could join them someone rushed out of the new building, where His Holiness was staying, and in a state of near panic informed Harry that water was not getting through to His Holiness's apartment. Consequently Harry had to stay behind and sort out the water problem while someone ran to get his wife Gwen to drive His Holiness into town. His Holiness arrived to find people in a state of commotion and on learning the reason for it burst into laughter and patted Harry on the head bestowing a blessing that more than compensated for his having to stay behind and dig up water pipes.

Harry had an inkling what the problem might be but in order to get it sorted out before His Holiness returned from Lockerbie he needed help with the digging. At first nobody volunteered then, as if by magic, Akong Rinpoche suddenly appeared, grabbed a pick axe and started to dig. Within minutes a team of people joined in and the work was completed with time to spare before a very happy Gwen drove up to return her precious passengers safely back to Samye Ling.

Whilst at Samye Ling His Holiness spent a few days up at the recently acquired nearby property known as Sevens, which would later become pert of the long term retreat complex.

36

One day Akong Rinpoche and Sherab Palden paid a visit to His Holiness who promptly decided they should do a kora, or circumambulation, of the house and surrounding land. There were many large rocks along the path, one of which His Holiness said was a particularly nice rock. Akong Rinpoche replied that it was just a rock but that if His Holiness would make a footprint on it then it would indeed become a special rock. His Holiness just laughed saying that Akong Rinpoche always said funny things. Nevertheless he did step on the rock. There was no footprint to be seen and everyone forgot the incident until some years later when the rock had to be moved during the building of the retreat centre. Some people wanted to get rid of the rock altogether but Rinpoche told them to keep it and when Sherab Palden's nephew Gyamtso washed the mud off it he discovered the clear imprint of His Holiness's foot.

Another couple in Samye Ling at that time was Ken and Katia Holmes. Katia, a young French woman who was a lecturer at a new university in Paris, had first heard about Samye Ling in 1969 and was intrigued enough to hitchhike to Scotland and find out what this Tibetan Buddhist Centre was all about. As an academic Katia had a rather intellectual approach to Buddhism, until she met Akong Rinpoche who promptly told her "No books!" Katia's health had long been problematic but Akong Rinpoche agreed to help her and gave her many physical and mental exercises to work with. A year later, Katia decided to take a sabbatical from her university and came to live at Samye Ling where she met Ken Holmes. Having received individual teachings from Akong Rinpoche they, and others members of the community, went on to receive further teachings from Kalu Rinpoche in 1974. It was after this memorable visit that many people, including Ken and Katia first started to formally practice the Ngondro, or Four Foundations.

By the time of His Holiness Karmapa's visit in 1977 Katia and Ken had started to learn some Tibetan. They also had the great good fortune to accompany His Holiness during his sixth month trip around Europe. Ken was the tour secretary and Katia acted as negotiator for His Holiness' projects to acquire land in the Dordogne. It was during this trip that His Holiness instructed Khenpo Tsultrim Gyamtso to teach Katia, Ken and others the Tibetan language. The schedule was tough but rewarding with the Khenpo's students required to learn each days' lessons by heart. It was also an awe inspiring time to be witnessing His Holiness' effect on people as he travelled around Europe giving so many precious teachings and performing the Black Crown Ceremony several times a week. Three months into the trip, while giving teachings in Belgium, His Holiness first asked Katia to translate for him. She was mortified and did not feel ready for such an important job. Nevertheless, she could hardly refuse His Holiness and so began her long career as a translator of Tibetan teachings and texts.

Ken remembers this precious time with His Holiness as being like accompanying the Buddha Himself. "He shone like the sun", recalls Ken, "It was totally uplifting to be in his presence. My memories range from experiencing the sublime spirituality of the Vajra Crown Ceremony, through his gentle way of handling and talking to birds, to him getting a Regent Street salesman to jump up and down on a suitcase, just as in the Samsonite TV commercial! Whatever he did was a teaching, bringing joy and meaning into our lives. Time and again we saw all those he met, be they Buddhists or non Buddhists, statesmen or ordinary people transported by his overwhelming presence into a state of joyful and unexpected openness. His compassion and confidence, born of supreme mastery, made even the most noted Buddhist teachers seem like children next to him. During those six months we witnessed this truly enlightened being manifesting his activity, firmly establishing the Dharma in new continents and briefly yet unforgettably illuminating the lives of countless people."

His Holiness' many discussions with Akong Rinpoche during this second visit led to the emergence of several important long term plans for Samye Ling. It had become apparent over the last ten years that, through the establishing of Samye Ling, Tibetan Buddhism had not only taken root in the UK but was also starting to grow and flourish. The concept of the Samye Project arose in answer to the need of directing and accommodating this response to Buddhism. In order to accomplish the next stage it was first necessary to provide a legal framework on which to base the Project.

With the help and legal expertise of longstanding friend and supporter of Samye Ling, Judge John Maxwell, the Karma Kagyu Trust was formed in Britain and an autonomous branch created at Samye Ling called Karma Drubgyud Darjay Ling, meaning, 'the place from which the teachings of the practice lineage spread and flourish'. With Akong Rinpoche appointed as its Abbot and Administrator, the scope of this Trust was much more comprehensive than the Johnstone House Trust and would allow the work of Samye Ling to expand and fulfil the needs of an increasing number of people coming to the Centre. It particularly facilitated the new Samye Project building scheme and the sponsoring of visiting Lamas from abroad. The two Trusts became closely affiliated and the Centre changed its official name to Kagyu Samye Ling. Thanks to the continued efforts of the Chairman of both Trusts, Judge John Maxwell, they have worked hand in hand to establish and further Buddhism in the UK.

The aims and objectives of the two Trusts are as follows:
• To provide a place of tranquillity and retreat where people of any faith may seek spiritual regeneration.
• To provide a forum where noted figures of religious and philosophical traditions may present and share their understanding.
• To teach the study and practice of Buddhism.
• To present and apply the teachings and practices of the Karma Kagyu school of Buddhism.
• To preserve Tibetan arts, medicine, philosophy, logic, metaphysics, astrology, sacred music, dance, crafts and skills.
• To establish Karma Kagyu Centres, schools, colleges, monasteries, nunneries, communities and retreats in the UK and elsewhere.
• To bring qualified Buddhist teachers, of any authentic tradition, to teach in these establishments.
• To provide libraries and facilities for the translation, printing, publishing and sale of texts, books, teachings and articles.
• To preserve holy relics, images and other sacred Tibetan objects.

Over the years the Trusts have augmented the original premises of Samye Ling, in order to accommodate growth, with the acquisition of nearby land and properties. The first of these was Fir Tree Lodge, a property just north of Johnstone House which included a fine pasture cum hayfield. With the later addition of an office/conference room this later became a working headquarters for Akong Rinpoche. The next place to become available was a rather unusual seven sided house, half a mile south of Samye Ling, which now forms part of the Purelands Retreat complex. Later on a small manor house called Moodlaw was purchased for the use of Centre staff with families and later still Garwald, another large house to the north of the Centre, was acquired as further accommodation for both residents and guest visitors.

The Samye Project itself was the combined vision of His Holiness Karmapa and Akong Rinpoche. Because of its rather ambitious nature the project was divided into several phases to be accomplished as time and funds permitted. The first and most essential part of the Project was to be the building of the Samye Ling temple. The shrine room in Johnstone House could no longer accommodate the amount of people wishing to practice and attend teachings, particularly when given by some of the most eminent Buddhist teachers of our time. The fact that the local village hall had to be hired as a venue for His Holiness to perform ceremonies illustrated how important it was to build a shrine room worthy of such exalted beings. People needed to be able to attend such teachings, prayers and ceremonies in an appropriate environment. Akong Rinpoche outlined his plans to His Holiness who immediately gave his blessing for the project and helped decide on a site for the new development.

The Samye Project as a whole would consist of Phase I, a large temple and shrine room on the ground floor with the lineage holders apartments, audience room and reliquary on the upper floors. This would be followed by Phase II which would house the Abbot's office, visiting and resident monks' quarters, a large refectory, kitchens and store rooms. Then finally Phase III which would consist of several small shrine rooms, Tibetan and English Libraries, College study and lecture facilities, a Museum, an Audio Visual studio and nuns' quarters. When complete the entire complex would form a quadrangle with the temple at one end and two L shaped wings adjoining it which would meet to form a grand gateway opposite the main shrine room.

Such an ambitious project would cost millions of pounds to realise. However, the only money available to Samye Ling at that time was a few thousand pounds made up of individuals' sponsorship donations. To engage professional building contractors would require large payments in advance or in instalments, which basically put it out of the question. Akong Rinpoche's solution was to get the Samye Ling residents themselves to build the temple. It was a brave and far sighted decision which meant that the temple could only be built as and when funds and the availability of skilled labour permitted.

Before work could begin on Phase I it was first necessary to gather together a skilled building team. Most of the able bodied residents at Samye Ling were university graduates with hardly anyone qualified in building skills. Akong Rinpoche was not to be deterred. He merely asked the volunteers where their interests lay and sent them away to get training in the appropriate skills. Vin Harris, for example, had left University with a degree in English Literature before coming to live at Samye Ling in 1975. As a resident he first worked on maintenance, after which he built an extension to the cow shed using found wood and then worked looking after the cows. When Akong Rinpoche asked him what skill he would like to learn that could help with building the temple Vin replied that he'd always been drawn to woodwork. Consequently he went to London and enrolled on a woodwork course at Hounslow Technical College.

Similarly, Nick Jennings went away and learnt blacksmithing and mechanics, Adrian Solomon did a course in bricklaying and Jerry Dowling was apprenticed by R and D Builders to learn all aspects of the building trade.

Meanwhile Akong Rinpoche worked with American architect Peter Lebasci who lived locally, and translated Rinpoche's plans and Sherab Palden's traditional Tibetan artistic knowledge into architectural drawings. Phase 1 of the Project was designed as a three storey building which would combine Tibetan architectural influences with modern materials and needs. The main temple would be on the ground floor and become the focus for Samye Ling's spiritual activities. The first floor would consist of apartments and audience rooms for the Kagyu lineage holders, while the top floor would house a smaller shrine cum reliquary, embellished by a pagoda style roof.

Planning permission was sought but not immediately forthcoming. There being no precedent for the construction of a Tibetan style temple in the Scottish borderlands the authorities and certain locals were initially wary. Eventually, some two years down the line, after the sympathetic intervention of local landowner Lord Tanlaw, coupled with extensive support from the media, planning permission was finally granted.

In 1979 the first spadefuls of earth were dug for the consecration ceremony performed by Lama Gendun, a great yogi and meditation master who presided over His Holiness' seat in the Dordogne area of France. Work could then begin in earnest with the digging of the foundations for the Samye Project temple, a job which was helped in no small measure by use of a JCB driven by David Hayward who borrowed the equipment from his father's building firm.

At various intervals in the ensuing months Samye Ling was visited by the revered heart sons of the Kagyu Lineage, namely Khentin Tai Situpa, Kunzik Sharmapa, Goshir Gyaltsapa, and Jamgon Kongtrul Rinpoche, each of whom placed sacred objects in specific areas of the foundations to add their blessings and truly provide a strong spiritual foundation for the work to follow. The resident community set to work with great enthusiasm and energy, inspired by the example of Akong Rinpoche himself who spent as much time as he could on the building site. Samye Ling became a veritable hive of activity with people of all nationalities, ages and abilities purposefully digging, mixing concrete, sawing wood, laying bricks and generally working together, bonded by their common aim to build a temple worthy of the Samye name.

As the building progressed workers passed on their knowledge to others and many people picked up valuable skills which were to serve them well later in life. One such person was Bernard Provost, a young French man who had come to Samye Ling in 1978, more out of curiosity than from any conscious spiritual quest. Bernard had a degree in horticulture and had also worked for his father as a commercial flower grower. When he first arrived at Samye Ling he naturally gravitated to working in the gardens and had been instrumental in starting the vegetable garden as well as helping with the flower gardens, digging the pond and landscaping the grounds. However, when the building work became a priority Bernard gave much of his time and energy to helping, particularly with the concreting and general building work. Over the following years he picked up enough knowledge and building skills to start his own building firm and currently employs nine people.

Once the building started to take shape and its oriental style roof become clearly visible just above the Eskdalemuir tree line, it began to attract a lot of attention from the media. Numerous articles appeared in national and international newspapers and various television crews descended on the newly emerging temple. One particularly in depth programme entitled 'Akong and the Big Shrine Room' was made for the prestigious First Tuesday series introduced by David Dimbleby. It gave a real sense of the dedication and community spirit engendered by Akong Rinpoche and his project. Many familiar faces are featured, including that of Vin Harris who was a key worker throughout the Project. Like Bernard, Vin has since put his acquired building skills to good use and now runs a successful business making and installing sash windows.

Both Bernard and Vin met their wives and started families at Samye Ling before building themselves homes and moving to nearby Eskdalemuir Village as their children grew older. Indeed it is through families such as theirs that the local village was given a new lease of life and the village school kept open. Although each of their families lives independently of Samye Ling they are both still very much involved with the Centre. Vin and Bernard still join in with various building projects, such as the recent construction of the prayer wheel house, while Marilyn Harris works for Akong Rinpoche's Rokpa Charity and also organises Buddhist funerals for members of the community who pass away. Sue Provost also comes to Samye Ling regularly and continues to lend her artistic skills to the painting and gilding of numerous beautiful statues, many of which can be seen adorning the main shrine room.

So many other people contributed their talents, energy and building skills to the development of Samye Ling and the creation of Phase I. While it would be virtually impossible to name them all this might be an appropriate time in the Samye Ling story to mention and thank some of the key contributors.

Principal Architect: Peter Labasci
Engineers, Architectural and Building Consultants: David Cameron, Peter Glass, David Hayward, Harry Milward, David Robinson.
General Builders, Masons, Plumbers, Electricians, Joiners, Metalworkers, Plasterers, Painters and Decorators: Ted Burkwall, Al Cope, Jerry Dowling, Alex Duncan, Andrew Gordon, Vin Harris, David Hayward, Don Henry, Nick Jennings, Lennie Jewitt, Sture Johannson, Erns Leeuwerink, Alan Sharples, Cameron Skillen, Josep Solers Monells, Adrian Solomon, Tsering Tashi, Oliver Tennyson, Will White, Marjan Wieringa, Pim Willems, Malcom Wylie.
Building Office Staff: Jeffrey Freeman, Kenneth Holmes, Rosemary Huston, Philip Johnson.

Thanks are also due to the support team of residents and visitors who helped selflessly with office work, cooking, cleaning, and other necessary jobs that allowed the building project to come to fruition. And finally we would like to thank the building inspectors Mr. Brown and Mr. Jardine for their years of help, and also Mr. Bell for giving his planning advice.

His Holiness the 16th Gyalwa Karmapa

His Holiness' official document naming Kagyu Samye Ling

His Holiness' footprint

H.H. the 16th Karmapa's meets the Pope at the Vatican, with Akong Rinpoche second from left

His Holiness
The Gyalwa Karmapa

July 3, 1977

KARMA KAGYU TRUST
KARMA DRUBGYUD DAR JAY LING

TO WHOM IT MAY CONCERN

THROUGH THE POWER GRANTED TO ME BY THE KARMA KAGYU TRUST, I HEREBY
APPOINT THE ABBOT OF TSAWA GANG DROLMA LHAKANG THE SECOND AKONG
RINPOCHE, KARMA SHETRUP CHOSGYI NYIMA TRINLEY KUNCHAB PAL ZANGPO
CHOLAY NAMPAR GYALWAY DAY, NOW KNOWN AS SHETRUP AKONG TARAP AS MY
REPRESENTATIVE, ABBOT AND DIRECTOR OF THE MONASTERIES AND RELIGIOUS
ORGANISATIONS TO BE ESTABLISHED UNDER THE KARMA DRUBGYUD DAR JAY LING.
KARMA DRUBGYUD DAR JAY LING WILL BE ESTABLISHED AT SAMYE LING, SCOT-
LAND, AND OTHER PARTS OF EUROPE.
SHETRUP AKONG TARAP SHALL HAVE COMPLETE AUTHORITY IN ALL MATTERS
CONCERNING THE ACTIVITIES AND ESTABLISHING OF KARMA DRUBGYUD DAR JAY
LING ORGANISATION.

WITH BLESSINGS AND PRAYERS

SIGNED AND SEALED BY HIS HOLINESS
THE XVITH GYALWA KARMAPA.

The Seats of His Holiness the Gyalwa Karmapa

Dharmachakra Centre	Tashi-Chöling	Karmaraj Vihara
Rumtek, Gangtok	Bumthang	Swayambhunath
Sikkim, India	Bhutan	Kathmandu Nepal

Cable Dharmachakra Centre Sikkim   Phone Gangtok 163

*His Holiness' appointment of Akong Rinpoche as his official
representative in the UK and Europe*

Building Samye Ling Temple

CHAPTER V

A FLOWERING OF ARTS

As the external structure of the Phase I progressed so too did the artwork destined to grace its interior. The work of producing these myriad objects served both to pass on the traditional skills involved to western students and to preserve the precious arts of Tibet for future generations. Under the direction of master artist Sherab Palden Beru numerous talented western artists and crafts people worked on the paintings, sculptures, carvings, mouldings and a host of other artifacts which would transform the empty shell of a building into the magnificent shrine room it is today. One of the first to arrive was Dolma Jeffries who had studied art at the Slade then got her MA at Reading before coming to Samye Ling in the early seventies. After a year of making beds, cleaning toilets and doing kitchen duties Dolma was apprenticed to Sherab Palden at the suggestion of Akong Rinpoche. As Sherab Palden's first western student Dolma had to earn his trust and spent many months cleaning brushes, tidying the studio, mixing pigments and most of all, observing the master at work.

Eventually Sherab Palden started giving Dolma drawings to do and as her talent became apparent she was allowed to paint small details on the thangkas. As she gradually assimilated the painstaking techniques of the Karma Gadri School, of which Sherab Palden was a leading exponent, Dolma was able to accomplish entire paintings. She was also able to bring her knowledge of western techniques and materials to help with the creation of artworks for the temple and introduced working with acrylics as a means of preventing the paintings from flaking. It was also her idea to paint the images, planned for the walls of the shrine room, on large canvases which could be moved around rather than as murals which might become damaged as the walls 'settled in.'

Other artists who have undertaken the long term commitment involved in studying and practising under Sherab Palden Beru have most notably included the German artist Heinz Hoes as well as Monica Tinley, Carlo Luyckx, Edith Irwin, and Babet Serrano. They were later followed by more recent students such as Ani Kunzang, Olivia Keir, Ani Semchi, Senge, Mikmar and Tsultrim, all of whom spent several years working in the exquisitely luminous style of the Karma Gadri School to produce an abundance of fine thangkas, many of which decorate the Samye Ling shrine room today. Thanks to the high quality photographs of Peter Mannox most of the thangkas produced at the Centre are reproduced in full colour and are available from the Samye Ling shop and mail order.

The influence of Sherab Palden Beru extends to every aspect of artistic creativity at Samye Ling and has guided such disciplines as wood carving, statue making, interior decoration and carpet weaving design. Many original pieces, first created under his direction in wood or clay, were then copied in resin whenever multiple items were required. This technique also preserves the designs for future use at Samye Ling or in other Centres and temples around the world.

The wealth of beautiful carvings to be seen in the temple started life as traditional forms and patterns drawn by Sherab Palden, sometimes directly onto the wood, before being carved out into three dimensional pieces. Using the straight grained fine textured jelutong wood from the forests of Malaysia a small group of highly skilled craftsmen would virtually bring Sherab Palden's drawings to life, creating dragons, birds, lions, lotus and mythological garudas surrounded by a rich profusion of flora and fauna twining around the shrines, thrones, cabinets and pillars of the temple. The main exponent of this highly specialised woodwork was an English Buddhist called Yeshe Tsultrim who came to live at Samye Ling in 1980. He was already an accomplished wood carver, having learnt his craft in both England and Germany. Yeshe was joined by Frenchman Joel Claude, aka Max, and a Tibetan monk called Yeshe Dorje who together made up the wood working team that crafted the multitude of fine carvings now gracing the Samye Ling temple to the delight of residents and guests alike.

Another important branch of artistic endeavour was the making and gilding of different types of statues, ranging from the imposing Buddha Sakyamuni that dominates the main shrine, to the thousand and eight miniature figures, representing each of the teaching Buddhas of our age, that surround it. Once again, Sherab Palden provided the beautifully proportioned drawings from which highly skilled craftspeople such as his nephew Tashi Gyamtso work in a variety of techniques to produce the various statues. A gifted artist in his own right, Gyamtso has contributed an enduring influence and prolific output of clay master originals for casting as well as numerous stone carvings found in Samye Ling and on Holy Island.

Ronald Long and John Chinnery worked on reproducing the small Buddha images from the early seventies, experimenting with different materials to produce various effects. By the mid to late seventies they were producing quite large figures, not only for Samye Ling but also for many other Dharma Centres. They were later joined by Marie Boysen, Madeleine Venturi and Alex Duncan. Apart from the creation of statues, the casting workshop team also manufactured a variety of decorative features used both inside and outside of the temple. Many new techniques and materials had to be developed to produce large quantities of the various types of images and decorations. Plaster, resin, and fibreglass were all used in the manufacturing process alongside the more traditional materials of wood and clay.

Most of the statuary was then painstakingly gilded in the gilding workshop. There the finishing touches would be applied to such diverse artworks as the exotic chu seng, or water dragons that look out from the four corners of the temple roof, down to the most delicate figures, such as those of Tara and Chenrezig, which would then be exquisitely painted. Early gilders and painters included Madeleine Venturini and Jill Farrier. Many others, too numerous to mention have followed suit over the years, until the present day when Sue Bradley, Ani Kunzang and Ashley Mago are currently carrying on the good work.

During the early eighties, as so many different items were being created to decorate and furnish the shrine room, a wide range of crafts and craftspeople gravitated to Samye Ling to fulfil the various needs. June Burley, who had learnt Tibetan carpet weaving from Tibetans in Nepal , set up looms at Samye Ling and taught several others the craft. They were joined by Akong Rinpoche's sister Sime Tarap and Nancy Chinnery, both accomplished weavers, who between them produced many beautiful carpets and wall hangings principally used in the High Lamas apartments.

A silk screening department was also set up in order to produce hundreds of decorative panels for the walls and ceiling of the temple. Traditionally in Tibet such work would have been hand painted by a team of monks taking many years to complete. With the silk screen technique two people were able to produce the elaborate phoenix and dragon ceiling panels, with their seventeen different colours, in a matter of months. Both Tsering Tashi and Lennie Jewitt had done silk screening before, but neither had tackled a job of such scale and complexity. Much research, experimentation and patient hard work went into the creation of the four hundred metre square panels that now grace the temple ceiling.

All the above mentioned artworks were created in a rather primitive looking collection of wooden workshops alongside a pottery which was started by Elizabeth McIntyre then run by Sonja Gerling, both of whom produced many fine pottery items. Another workshop housed the print room, started by Craig Gibson and Clive Holmes as a means to reproduce Sherab Palden's beautiful artwork by carving lino blocks and printing them by hand. Such were the simple beginnings of what later became a sophisticated print shop equipped with modern machinery able to produce English and Tibetan texts, and many kinds of printed material.

This outpouring of creative arts flourished in tandem with the building of Samye Project Phase I. Everyone contributed their particular skill towards the fulfilment of Akong Rinpoche's dream. The people mentioned above were some of the key artists involved, but they are only a fraction of all those who helped. It is said in many scriptures that to build temples and places where wisdom, truth and compassion flourish generates incalculable virtue which will continue for 'as long as even one stone or brick of the building exists.' Therefore all those who directly or indirectly contributed to the Samye Project have participated in a wonderful undertaking and most wholesome act of goodness. Everyone connected with the Project will eventually benefit greatly, not just in this life but in many lives to come.

Jean Claude

Oliver Tennyson

Nick Jennings

48

Artist Dolma Jeffries

Weavers, June Burleigh and Sime

49

Sherab Palden and Akong Rinpoche

Rinpoche at work

Tashi Gyamtso

Master artist Sherab Palden Beru

CHAPTER VI

INNER DEVELOPMENT

While Akong Rinpoche was busy overseeing the building of the Samye Ling temple his younger brother Jamdrak had been equally busy on the other side of the Atlantic where he had successfully set up and managed the Karma Triyana Dharmachakra Centre in New York State. The erstwhile pleasure seeking rebel had evolved into the hardworking and well respected treasurer of His Holiness the Karmapa's main seat in the US, so much so that Akong Rinpoche asked him to return to the UK to help run Samye Ling.

Jamdrak however, felt the need to work on himself further before he could really be in a position to help others. He decided to become a monk and to enter a strict solitary retreat. Accordingly, when His Holiness Karmapa was visiting the US in 1980 Jamdrak asked to be ordained. His Holiness bestowed full Gelong ordination on the auspicious date commemorating the Buddha's Parinirvana in a special ceremony attended by nine High Lamas of the Kagyu Lineage.

Under his ordination name Yeshe Losal, the new monk offered all his worldly wealth to His Holiness then entered into a strict solitary retreat in a wood cabin in the grounds of the KTD Centre. He saw nobody apart from his teacher Khenpo Kartha and occasionally High Lamas such as Kalu Rinpoche and Jamgon Kongtrul who gave him valuable advice and instructions on various practices. With strict diligence and boundless energy Yeshe Losal threw himself wholeheartedly into his practice, determined to make up for his past mistakes and taking for his example and inspiration the renowned Tibetan yogi Milarepa.

Meanwhile, back at Samye Ling a group of western practitioners were preparing to enter the first closed retreat of its kind in the UK. On his last visit to Samye Ling His Holiness the 16th Karmapa had discussed plans with Akong Rinpoche for the provision of a long term retreat that would give serious Buddhist practitioners the opportunity to further their practice within the traditional Tibetan framework of the three year, three month, three week retreat. He had also visited the proposed site for the retreat, which was adjacent to the house known as Sevens. Thereafter the place became known as Purelands.

When Akong Rinpoche, accompanied by many people from Samye Ling, made a pilgrimage to the holy Buddhist sites in India, he held further discussions with His Holiness Karmapa. As a result of these meetings it was decided to begin the first long retreat at Purelands in 1984. This would give future participants enough time to raise the necessary funds and also prepare themselves by studying Tibetan language and various recommended texts.

The retreat was to be run along traditional lines and introduce western students to all the main practices of the Kagyu Lineage, starting with the Four Foundations, through to the various Guru Yogas, the yidam practices, and the Six Yogas of Naropa. In order to allow for the difficulties with language and the newness of this kind of retreat in the West it was decided to extend the length of the retreat from the usual three years and three months to a period of four years. This would also allow time for the practices of Guru Rinpoche and of Amitabha which Akong Rinpoche considered would be of great benefit in enriching the lives of all the retreatants.

On his return to Samye Ling Akong Rinpoche told all those interested in participating of his plans regarding this first retreat. One of those people was a young Danish woman called Elise Jacobsen. Elise had been living at Samye Ling since 1977 after having taken Refuge with His Holiness Karmapa. When not working in the dairy making butter and cheese she would attend many of the teachings given by High Lamas during that time, including those of the four precious Heart Sons of the Kagyu Lineage. By the time Akong Rinpoche made his announcement about the forthcoming long retreat Elise was working in Rinpoche's office photocopying texts. When Rinpoche asked her if she would like to do the retreat, even though there was no precedent and she didn't know what to expect, she found herself saying "yes." Consequently, she returned to Denmark and worked as a kindergarten assistant teacher and as a cleaner in order to raise the necessary funds.

In March 1984 Akong Rinpoche formally closed the boundaries as nine women and seven men entered their respective houses, at the Purelands Retreat, to begin the first ever long term closed retreat in the UK. Lama Ganga was the Retreat Master presiding over this ground breaking initiative, acting as both teacher and counsellor to the western students in his care. It was a multi-national group with people from many European countries and beyond. On entering, the retreatants took vows similar to those of monks and nuns and when Khenchen Thrangu Rinpoche later bestowed ordination in 1985 many of them elected to take robes, including Elise who became the nun Ani Zangmo. Still others entered the sangha when His Eminence Tai Situpa gave a further ordination in 1987.

Everything was very new to the retreatants. There were not yet many translations available, some of the Tibetan texts were poorly printed and difficult to read, nobody had experience of rituals such as the making of torma offerings or playing sacred music, indeed it was a totally unprecedented situation for everyone concerned. However, one thing the retreat pioneers did have was a wealth of teachings and empowerments from the most noted Buddhist Masters of modern times. Thanks to the great kindness of Akong Rinpoche the retreat was visited in 1984 by His Holiness the Dalai Lama, in 1987 by the Venerable Kalu Rinpoche, and was regularly visited by His Eminence Tai Situpa, Khenchen Thrangu Rinpoche, and also Lama Thubten and Lama Lodro all of whom gave precious teachings which augmented those of Retreat Master, Lama Ganga. The instructions and inspiration afforded by contact with these exceptional beings more than made up for the students' basic living conditions and lack of experience.

On one memorable day in the summer of 1984 as Ani Zangmo was tidying up in the women's shrine room, Akong Rinpoche suddenly turned up carrying a strange piece of equipment which turned out to be a bomb detector. Rinpoche casually explained that this was a routine part of the security procedures taken before His Holiness the Dalai Lama was allowed to enter a building, whether it was a Retreat Centre or not. The young nun's jaw dropped as this was the first she'd heard of His Holiness' visit. An hour later His Holiness was sitting on the throne in the women's retreat house surrounded by a small group of incredulous but ecstatic retreatants who could hardly believe their eyes. It was as if the Buddha himself had suddenly manifested in their modest shrine room.

After giving the retreat members advice and blessings His Holiness returned to Samye Ling where the main activities of his three day visit included blessing the semi built temple and giving a public talk on Mahayana Buddhism with its emphasis on the merits of unconditional love and compassion. His Holiness's talk was delivered inside the half built shell of the new shrine room with a huge white sheet providing a simple back drop and swallows flying in and out during the teaching. It was the first teaching ever held inside the temple and a very auspicious start for all the dharma activities to follow. His Holiness also helped Akong Rinpoche choose a site on which to build a stupa, a sacred monument, where he blessed the ground and cut a symbolic turf. On his last day His Holiness was guest of honour at a crowded garden party where he cut a huge cake and delighted all comers with his great charm, simplicity and good humour.

The last year of the retreat saw the arrival of another unexpected visitor. The first sign of the new arrival was a flurry of activity in the seven sided house adjacent to the men's and women's retreat houses. Caretakers were cleaning the place and stocking it with food ready to receive non other than Akong Rinpoche's brother Yeshe Losal.

After already completing five years of intensive solitary retreat in the US Yeshe Losal intended to carry on with many more years in retreat. However, Akong Rinpoche had invited their other brother and sister over from Tibet and as they were unable to obtain visas to go to America, Akong Rinpoche requested Lama Yeshe Losal to interrupt his retreat in order to meet them. Although he had not seen his brother and sister since leaving Tibet in 1959 Yeshe Losal was reluctant to break his retreat by travelling to the UK. His reluctance was not because he didn't wish to see his family but because he held the precious practice of Buddha Dharma above all personal considerations. Finally a compromise was reached when Akong Rinpoche promised Yeshe Losal that he would be able to continue his retreat at Purelands.

The person who arrived at Samye Ling in 1987 was altogether different from the one who had left for the US so many years before. Outwardly he had metamorphosed from a fashion conscious, Afro haired rebel to a burgundy robed, shaven headed monk with not much flesh on his bones after years of intensive, one-pointed practice. Samye Ling too had changed in the intervening years. The new building guest accommodation block was up and the Samye temple almost finished. After a joyous reunion with his long lost family Yeshe Losal once more entered into retreat.

Although he was living up at the Purelands Retreat Centre Yeshe Losal had his own house and was able to continue his solitary retreat practice. However, he would also spend time helping the western retreat members, particularly when Lama Ganga had to go away. The fact that he had so much experience with young western people, combined with his great aptitude as a meditator made Yeshe Losal ideally placed to give guidance to the men and women in retreat. His joy and exuberance were inspiring and gave the group a tremendous lift during the latter stages of their retreat. He particularly helped with the translation of the Six Yogas of Naropa and gave group talks and individual interviews to all those who sought his advice. When the group retreat was completed in the spring of 1988 and Akong Rinpoche came to formally open the boundaries Yeshe Losal remained in his solitary retreat. All the Western retreatants came out and for the first time in four years the men and women, who had been undergoing the same experiences in such close proximity without seeing each other, were finally able to meet. They then made a procession down to Samye Ling where they were reunited with their families and friends. It was a memorably happy occasion but somewhat overwhelming both for the people who had been in retreat and for those who came to greet them. Akong Rinpoche advised everyone not to have too high expectations and to see this first retreat as a time of learning rather than have unrealistic ideas about enlightenment. Nevertheless he said it had been a most beneficial experience, not only for the participants but also for their families and supporters who had made it possible.

There was already a waiting list for the next long retreat, which was planned to start in the spring of the following year, with many of the first time retreatants committing themselves to do a second retreat. However, with a total of twenty five men and twenty women signed up the retreat facilities had to be considerably enlarged. As the actual building work on the Samye temple had now finished, leaving the painters and decorators to complete the job, the building team were able to move on to Purelands and turn their attention to building new retreat houses for the men and women. The builders were augmented by many of the future retreatants who came to lend a hand so that the houses could be finished in time.

Diggers and other heavy machinery shattered the peace of the once tranquil Purelands where Yeshe Losal was still in deep retreat. His porch was used as a dry store room for bags of plaster whose dust crept in under his door, irritating his one good lung. The noise of machinery and people shouting instructions was almost deafening but in true Vajrayana tradition he used all these seeming obstacles to further his practice by reminding himself how this building work was such a positive thing. It would allow many more of his western Vajra brothers and sisters to practice Buddha Dharma for the benefit of beings.

In March 1989, with the paint barely dry inside the hurriedly built new houses, the second long retreat began after Akong Rinpoche had once more closed the boundaries. In the intervening months between the first and second retreats Lama Ganga, the previous Retreat Master, had travelled to Tibet and unfortunately passed away. Akong Rinpoche had no qualms about appointing Lama Yeshe Losal as the new Retreat Master. His experience in meditation retreat and his ability to communicate with western students made him ideal for the job. The situation was also a little easier as nine of the first retreats' participants had elected to join the second one. Among the men Irishman Donal Creedon, also known as Karma Tenzin, and the Spanish monk Jinpa were able to bring their experience to help and on the women's side Ani Zangmo and Ani Tsondreu did the same.

The second retreat continued along the same lines as the previous one albeit with some improvements based on experience, better texts and more translations, thanks to the work of Peter Roberts . His Eminence Tai Situpa and Khenchen Thrangu Rinpoche were the principal visiting High Lamas who bestowed all the necessary empowerments and teachings at various times throughout the retreat. The retreat came to a successful conclusion in the spring of 1993 and was then followed by a third retreat from November 1993 until 1997. Once again, Karma Tenzin and Ani Zangmo looked after the male and female retreatants respectively.

The acquisition of Holy Island for the purpose of building a new Retreat Centre and an interfaith Centre for World Peace and Health then meant a break of several years before the fourth and most recent retreat could begin. Eventually the first long retreat for women on Holy Island began in autumn 2002 and was completed in the spring of 2006. The men's retreat had to begin rather later to allow time to finish building their retreat house at Glenscorrodale on the Isle of Arran. It eventually started in the summer of 2005 and is still in progress at the time of writing. More information about Holy Island and Glenscorrodale is to be found in Chapter XI. Suffice it to say that each of these retreats built on the experiences of the previous ones and allowed some hundred and twenty people in total to participate in these precious opportunities.

*His Holiness the Dalai Lama
with Akong Rinpoche*

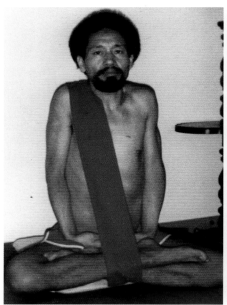

Lama Yeshe Losal in retreat

Akong Rinpoche and Lama Ganga at Purelands Retreat

Purelands Retreat

CHAPTER VII

MATURATION

Hardly had the ceremonies following the conclusion of the first long retreat abated when preparations for a vastly larger celebration began to gather pace. The official opening of the newly built Samye Ling temple was scheduled for the auspicious date of the 8/8/88. That particular date was significant for a number of reasons. Firstly it marked the 1000th anniversary of Tilopa, one of the principal forefathers of the Kagyu Lineage, secondly it was the 1200th anniversary of the original Samye in Tibet and thirdly it was the 21st anniversary of Samye Ling itself. In the months leading up to the special day activities at the centre shifted into top gear in a huge effort to put the finishing touches to the temple and get everything ready for the month of festivities which would culminate in the grand opening.

Although the main construction had already been completed there was still a wealth of detail to finish on the interior décor. Samye Ling became a frenzied hive of activity with an army of craftspeople frantically carving, gilding, painting and performing countless other tasks during those hectic summer months. Apart from finishing the shrine room there was also much work to do on the upper floors of the building which housed an apartment, audience room and shrine for the head of the Kagyu Lineage as well as a holy reliquary on the topmost floor.

As His Holiness the 16th Karmapa had passed away in 1981 and the 17th Karmapa had not yet been found, the four Heart Sons of the Lineage became Regents who were acting on his behalf. All the Regents had visited Samye Ling and given precious teachings but His Eminence Tai Situpa had been particularly active in the development of Samye Ling's spiritual progress and had regularly given teachings and empowerments, both in the closed retreats and in public. Akong Rinpoche therefore invited Tai Situpa to preside over the official opening in August, along with the celebrated Member of Parliament and long term supporter of Samye Ling Lord David Steel. However, Rinpoche had also asked Tai Situpa to perform the spiritual consecration of the building in advance of the opening which meant that the upper floor apartment had to be ready by July in order to accommodate His Eminence and his entourage.

At the same time as all the decorative work was in progress so were preparations for the ceremonies that would be performed during the consecration and the opening. Sherab Palden taught Dakini and Ani dances to a group of western women while the Venerable Gyamtso taught Lama dances to the men. Sherab's student Dolma Jeffries was one of the women doing the Dakini dancing but had to fit her dance practice in between sculpting heads for the main Buddha statue and for the Karmapa statue, both of which had to be ready in time for the consecration.

Last minute adjustments were being made right up to the day of Situ Rinpoche's arrival. Both Situ Rinpoche and Thrangu Rinpoche came to take part in the consecration and also lend their help and advice in the preceding weeks. Situ Rinpoche even climbed up to the very top of the temple roof in order to place some sacred relics in the bumpa, or ceremonial vase, that forms the pinnacle. He also painted in the eyes of the main Buddha causing it to become 'awake', after having filled the statue with many sacred objects.

When the day of the consecration ceremony dawned Dolma finally finished the statue of the 16th Karmapa and gave it to Akong Rinpoche to place on the Karmapa's throne in the temple. It was as if the Karmapa himself was sitting there, flanked by Situ Rinpoche on one side and Thrangu Rinpoche on the other as they presided over the ceremony and enjoyed the women's Dakini dance followed by the men's Mahakala dance. All the elaborately carved and painted masks and beautiful brocade costumes had been made at Samye Ling. It was a proud moment for the community to see all their efforts come together in a colourful spectacle of sacred music and dance in the wonderful new shrine room. The celebration represented not only the hard work and dedication of all concerned but also the transference of many precious arts and skills from Tibetan masters to western students.

After the consecration it was business as usual. There were still many finishing touches to put to the temple before the official opening day on August 8th. Visitors started to arrive from around the UK and abroad, all eager to lend a hand. Some of the resident community gave up their rooms for the visitors and camped out in tents in the field next to the temple. The first week in August was particularly wet and the unseasonable rain did not help matters. However, on the morning of the opening day itself the hot summer sun shone down from a clear blue sky as hundreds of guests began to converge on Samye Ling.

The new temple with its freshly painted, brightly coloured woodcarvings and golden roof sparkled in the brilliant sunlight as a crowd of more than 1,500 people gathered in the forecourt to witness the opening ceremony. The stirring tones of Tibetan jahlings trumpeted a fanfare as Lord David Steel, a dashing figure in the mufti of his Privy Councillor uniform, stepped up alongside His Eminence Tai Situpa to unveil the marble plaque set into the front wall of the temple. Akong Rinpoche, the driving force behind the whole project, managed to look both modest yet resplendent in a traditional yellow silk chuba as he quietly surveyed the scene. Although his outward expression was one of utter calm and equanimity he must surely have allowed himself a moment of satisfaction and pride in the accomplishment of the Samye Ling community who had laboured for nine long years to realise his vision.

One can only imagine the reaction of the visitors as they entered the temple for the first time to find themselves in the magnificent scarlet and gold shrine room, its walls embellished with huge, exquisitely painted thangkas and its rows of ornately carved columns leading to the beautiful shrine at the north end where the great golden Buddha gazes down with an expression of pure compassion. A constant flow of people wound around the room to take in the wealth of artistic detail adorning the thirty eight metre hall, from the main Buddha flanked by two sinuous dragons clutching wish fulfilling gems, to the one thousand and eight small Buddhas representing each teaching Buddha of our age.

As streams of people emerged from the shrine room to make their way down the temple steps the music of a Tibetan folk band rang out from the stage in an open sided, traditional Tibetan tent that had been erected in front of the temple. A troupe of gifted dancers from the Tibetan Institute of Performing Arts whirled around the stage in their national dress, like a flock of exotic birds weaving a blur of rainbow coloured patterns. The festivities continued throughout the day, speeches were made praising the amazing accomplishment of Akong Rinpoche, Sherab Palden and the Samye Ling community and their nine year labour of love in creating a £1.5 million building for less than a quarter of the cost through sheer hard work and dedication.

A sprinkling of well known faces were among the international, multi faith crowd that day and many others sent their messages of support and congratulations, including the Indian Prime Minister Rajiv Gandhi, Her Royal Highness Princess Margaret, the Chief Rabbi, the Archbishop of Canterbury, the Moderator of the Church of Scotland and a host of other leaders and celebrities. H.E. Tai Situpa, Akong Tulku Rinpoche and Lord Steel then joined hands to cut a mammoth cake, handsomely decorated with a large, edible, gold leaf key to be distributed among the happy throng as the day was rounded off with a sumptuous tea party.

One week after the Samye Project inauguration festivities a rather lower key but equally significant event brought the month long celebrations to a close. A three day Interfaith Symposium drew representatives from all the major faiths to a conference on the subject of Compassion through Understanding. The delegates discovered their similarities and discussed their differences in an atmosphere of tolerance and goodwill. They also took the opportunity to attend a Buddhist prayer service and a Christian eucharist held in the newly finished shrine room. The conference was the first of its kind to be held at Samye Ling but Akong Rinpoche expressed his intention to make it the forerunner of many such dialogues.

The inauguration of the Samye Ling temple represented the accomplishment of the first stage of Samye Project. The shrine room became the nucleus for daily dharma activities, prayer services and meditation sessions for residents and visitors. With the incorporation of floor to ceiling sliding screens the long rectangular hall could be divided into three sections for day to day use. The largest section contains the main shrine room and the two lesser sections consist of a smaller shrine room for individual practice and another room which is used for weekend workshops and therapies such as Tai Chi or Yoga. When visiting High Lamas come to give teachings and empowerments the screens can be slid back to open up the full length of the hall, which can then hold up to five hundred people.

His Holiness the Dalai Lama

Finishing touches to the temple

Lord David Steel and His Emminence Tai Situpa at the opening ceremony

Tibetan folk dancers

Crowds flock to the opening ceremony

THOUSANDS GATHER AS EUROPE'S LARGEST BUDDHIST TEMPLE OPENS

CULTURAL and religious differences were almost all forgotten as Europe's largest Buddhist temple at Eskdalemuir was officially opened this week.

The ceremony on the 'lucky' date, 8/8/88, brought together around 2000 invited guests to the Kagyu Samye Ling Tibetan Centre from the full spectrum of beliefs in East and West.

As rabbis mixed with archbishops and kirk ministers with Hinduise, the one dissenting voice came from a Free Church of Scotland member who claims his 'peaceful poster protest' against Buddhism in the borders was halted by police.

But the main business of the day was the official opening of the imposing and colourful temple by former Liberal Party leader David Steel, MP, and buddhist leader, The Khentin Tai Situpa.

The remarkable building, in traditional Tibetan style, has been superbly crafted and richly decorated with an eight-feet high gold Buddha image as centre piece of the shrine room which has accommodation for 600 people.

On upper floors there are appartments for visiting Buddhist leaders, an audience room and a reliquary of precious artifacts.

Efforts

The temple represents nine years of unpaid work by the hundred residents of the centre and the many visitors. Their efforts have meant that the building, valued at £1.5 million, was actually completed for £300,000.

But as Kenneth Holmes, secretary to the two administering charitable trusts, explained in his introduction, the temple is the first phase of a two part project with the next goal being the completion of a college and accommodation building and court yard.

He told the guests, including diplomats, local and national politicians: "Your presence here is a much appreciated sign that our work in preserving and presenting Tibet's religious, artistic and cultural heritage has been received in a spirit of friendship and understanding".

He then introduced the twin trusts' chairman John Maxwell, a Birmingham-based barrister and long-standing buddhist who has been involved with Eskdalemuir for 20 years.

Said Mr Maxwell: "Any stranger who comes here will surely think we have had colossal sponsorship from huge industrial concerns to raise the money to build a temple like this. In fact it was started with about £15.

● The golden Buddha image in the shrine room.

"This area was a hill of solid rock with trees on it. There wasn't even enough money to buy a JCB to level it. We started off with pick axes, shovels and wheel barrows".

He said there had been many generous donations but the temple would not have been possible without the volunteer workforce and the inspiration given by the abbot and administrator, Akong Rinposhe.

"It is quite obvious", he said, "that if people give up their jobs, give up their careers and come and stay here for no pay and just devote themselves to building a place like this there must have been some rather special inspiration".

He said Akong Rinposhe had also been an inspiration to others all over the world in setting up new centres. He was currently negotiating with the Chinese government to rebuild monasteries and provide new hospitals and schools in Tibet.

In his address, the abbot said that the temple was not important as a building. What was important was that through the project people were working together and "doing something useful for each other".

Dumfries and Galloway Regional Council convenor John Jameson said that the authority welcomed the community making their home in the region and their contribution to education.

Priority

He said: "Education throughout peoples lives is an absolute priority. We appreciate very much the type of education you give; not necessarily training for jobs — but training for people to live good lives".

Tai Situpa, Patriarch of the Karma Kagyu Buddhist tradition, described the

event as 'significant and important'.

He explained that the original Samye monastery — the first in Tibet — was opened around 1200 years ago and played a very important role.

And he added: "I believe this temple will play a similar role".

Mr Steel was dressed for the ceremony in the uniform of a privy councillor, originally worn by a member of Lloyd George's government.

He said the centre had enhanced the already beautiful surroundings and the community had brought its own blessings to the valley.

Said Mr Steel, who lives at Ettrick Bridge: "At a material level trade and tourism have increased because of your expansion. Many's the foreign visitor we get wending their way up Ettrick and stopping to ask how far it is to the monastery.

"The growing population means that the local school is also thriving".

The centre, he said, provided study, retreat and medication facilities for Buddhist and non-Buddhist alike.

Spiritual

"The centre's aims", he pointed out, "have been expressed very simply. They are to increase mental and physical wellbeing in the world and also preserve the rich spiritual and cultural heritage of Tibet".

Mr Steel said he was grateful that as a committed member of another faith he had been asked to perform the opening but added: "Given the sublime nature of your faith it is not surprising".

He continued: "For Buddhism above all is the epitome of tolerance and compassion. Two qualities which are sadly lacking and are deeply needed in all areas of our life today".

NEW ERA DAWNS FOR BORDER BUDDHISTS

● CROWDS converged on the tiny Dumfriesshire village of Eskdalemuir this week to see the opening of Europe's largest Buddhist temple.

The ceremony marked the successful conclusion of a nine-year labour of love by residents and visitors to the Samye Ling Buddhist Centre.

Friday, 12th August, 1988 — THE ANNANDALE OBSERVER 23

● CUTTING the 21st birthday cake, left to right: Kuentin Tai Situpa, David Steel and Akong Rinposhe.

36 – The Universe, Sunday August 14 1988

● Buddhist monks play a fanfare on traditional Tibetan instruments for the inauguration of their new temple in Scotland.

FANFARE FOR SCOTLAND'S BUDDHISTS

THE largest Tibetan Buddhist temple in Europe was officially opened this week in the Scottish Borders.

Archbishop O'Brien of Edinburgh and Bishop Taylor of Galloway were among the 2,000 guests and visitors who attended the ceremony in the tiny village of Eskdalemuir in Dumfriesshire.

Work on the Kagyu Samye Ling centre, built in traditional Tibetan style, began ten years ago. It houses 10 monks and 90 lay volunteers and is open for retreats to people of Christian and other faiths. After the ceremony Archbishop O'Brien described the temple as "very impressive".

"What was even more impressive was the reception from the monks. It was an open and friendly day reflecting the peace which the monks preach by their way of life".

The centre was inaugurated on the eighth day of the eighth month 1988 – one of the luckiest days of the century for Buddhists.

63

Interfaith Symposium at Samye Ling 1988

CHAPTER VIII

HEALTH

In addition to the blossoming of dharma activities at Samye Ling two other areas of Akong Rinpoche's work, namely health and charity, were also beginning to flower. Since its inception Samye Ling had been a place where people came for help to heal themselves of the stresses and sufferings of life. Akong Rinpoche's training in Tibetan medicine, allied with his compassion and selfless motivation to help all beings resulted in his being always ready to lend an ear and listen to people's problems in the fullest sense of the word. Often just the listening itself would help people find their own solutions. But if not, then Rinpoche had the wisdom to help each person in a myriad of ways according to their individual needs.

For many years this help was dispensed in an informal way, whether through private interviews or public teachings. Then, in 1980 Akong Rinpoche gave his first formal therapy course at Samye Ling in which he explained the Tibetan method of holistic healing. Several western therapists attended and as a result of his contact with them, a more structured form of therapy evolved combining Buddhist meditation and visualisation techniques with western methods such as massage, relaxation, art therapy, writing and reflection. Working with western therapists such as Edie Irwin, Carol Sagar, Dr. Brion Sweeney and Dorothy Gunne, Akong Rinpoche devised a system of therapy that has helped countless people over the years.

Edie Irwin had trained as a psychotherapist with R.D.Laing and had also worked in the Tibetan Refugee camp in Darjeeling. She first came to Samye Ling in 1977 where she studied thangka painting under Sherab Palden. She also attended many Buddhist teachings and used her previous training to help people through relaxation and massage. When Akong Rinpoche asked her what she did and Edie replied "massage" Rinpoche said he too did massage, adding "Compassion is the only massage that works." As Edie later elaborated, "Compassion is the beginning, middle and end of what Rinpoche means by therapy".

Later in 1980, when a group of regular visitors to Samye Ling wished to set up their own Centre in Edinburgh, Akong Rinpoche suggested that its primary activity should be therapy and that Edie should oversee the project. A property was rented as a base of operations where meditation sessions and therapy work could take place while Centre members began raising funds and generating income through holding workshops. Following the four lines of instruction she received from Akong Rinpoche, Edie set up Tara Rokpa in Edinburgh running courses called Beginning to Relax.

1986 saw the formation of the Edinburgh Tara Trust which, two years later, acquired its first property with income from therapy courses and private donations. Similar work was going on in other countries, notably in South Africa, where Professor Rob Nairn and Trish Swift were key people, and in Ireland where psychologists Dr. Brion Sweeney and Dorothy Gunne became involved. Carol Sagar, the art therapist from Norfolk also came on board and in the summer of '88 all the aforementioned gathered at Samye Ling to receive therapy teachings from Akong Rinpoche.

The group were actually evolving a form of psychotherapy, by participating in their own healing process, which was gently guided by Rinpoche who would give them various exercises to do including writing their lives backwards from the present to as far back as they could remember. They would meet with Rinpoche every evening and the next stage of the process would emerge organically according to the needs and skills of the individuals concerned. In this way a unique type of psychotherapy was born from a synthesis of the Tibetan healing system, with its profound Buddhist perspective, and a complimentary mix of tried and tested western therapies.

Over time these methods were refined and taught in many of Samye Ling's satellite Centres that had started to mushroom up in various countries around the world. Tape recordings of these teachings were gathered together by Edie and by Clive Holmes who eventually edited them into books, notably Taming the Tiger and Back to Beginnings, which have since sold many thousands of copies and been translated into several languages. Akong Rinpoche's vision of using western therapy rooted in Buddhist understanding, to create a healing process manifesting as compassion in action, has unfolded on a global scale.

In 1993 the Tara Rokpa Therapy Training was established to teach a growing number of therapists who wished to train in the system and by 2001 two four year training courses had been completed. With ten graduate Rokpa therapists actively practising and helping hundreds of people through their work the next step was to fully authenticate the Tara Rokpa Therapy as a valid method of psychotherapy able to be practiced in the UK and Europe. This was achieved in 2004 by a unanimous vote within the UK Council for Psychotherapy, enabling Tara Rokpa to award therapists its own certificate of training. An up to date list of Tara Rokpa branches and therapists around the world is available in Chapter XVII.

Anyone wishing to participate in Tara Rokpa Therapy can join whichever group is nearest to them. It is also possible to attend one of the introductory weekend workshops held several times throughout the year at Samye Ling. Participants can then go on to join a group for as much of the therapy programme as they find useful. In its entirety the whole process covers seven to eight years and consists of the following components: Learning to Relax, Back to Beginnings, Working with the Elements, Taming the Tiger, The Six Lights, The Six Realms, The Compassion Stage.

Akong Rinpoche encourages all who continue to the last stage to spend some of their time actively engaged in charitable and humanitarian work. This not only benefits those on the receiving end of charity but equally those who are able to offer it. As Rinpoche says, "Charity with wisdom, the highest form of charity, has no giver, no receiver and nothing to receive. It is pure, unconditional giving."

Another important aspect of Akong Rinpoche's work in the field of health is the preservation of Tibetan medicine. The science of healing in the Tibetan tradition covers much more than pharmaceutical medicine. It includes anything and everything that can transform discomfort into ease, sickness into health and despair into contentment. Tibetan medicine arose as a combination of the best of the Chinese and Indian systems in conjunction with its own vast body of knowledge and a pharmacopeia largely based on natural plants, minerals and extracts.

The Buddhist understanding of the interdependence of all things also plays a significant role in the diagnosis and treatment of mental and physical sickness, which is seen to be caused by imbalance and disharmony. These in turn are caused by the 'three poisons' of ignorance, craving and anger which form the basis of the egotism obscuring our true, enlightened nature. Chasing what we desire and running away from what we dislike causes imbalance and eventually sickness, although the causes and effects of this process may be spread over many years, or even lifetimes. On a macrocosmic level we see the same forces at work as mankind's ignorance and greed cause environmental degradation leading to ecological imbalance which manifests as climatic disasters and new strains of disease. Tibetan Medicine employs a variety of subtle and wholly natural means to identify the root causes of sickness, treat it and restore balance in a holistic manner.

In 1993 the Tara Rokpa College of Tibetan Medicine was established by the Rokpa Trust, in conjunction with the Institute of Tibetan Medicine in Lhasa. The aim of the college is to preserve the precious knowledge of Tibetan Medicine and to make it available to the world by teaching it to western medical practitioners. A four year study course, led by such eminent Tibetan physicians as Khenpo Troru Tsenam and Dr. Trogawa Rinpoche, was set up to provide western doctors and therapists with the opportunity to assimilate and apply this precious knowledge for the benefit of beings. To date there have been two such courses in Tibetan medicine with some forty people having completed the course.

In addition, Rokpa has sponsored the visits of a series of Tibetan doctors who have been able to treat a large number of patients over the years who would not otherwise have had access to this unique form of healing. The present incumbent is Dr. Lobsang Dhonden who divides his time between Edinburgh, Glasgow, London Samye Dzong and Samye Ling, holding clinics in each place on a monthly basis. It is largely due to Rokpa's work that Tibetan medicine has been officially recognised in the UK and Europe and is now able to benefit many more people.

Akong Tulku's work has helped people with both mental and physical health problems in a variety of ways. One of his most successful projects in the field of mental health was made possible through the Rokpa Trust's acquisition of Lothlorien as a place where people with mental health problems could live, work and regain their stability. A large and charmingly rustic log cabin set in spacious grounds serves as a residence for upto eight people living alongside therapists and carers. The therapeutic community of Lothlorien has an innovative approach which creates an atmosphere of mutual support that helps people regain their balance and confidence. Details of the Lothlorien community can be found in the Tara Rokpa section of Chapter XVII.

Tara Rokpa

Dr Dhonden and patient

Medicinal herb processing in Tibet

The garden at Lothlorien

CHAPTER IX

CHARITY

Although compassion and generosity had always been the motivating forces behind the work carried out at Samye Ling, it was the formation of the Rokpa Charitable Trust that enabled this work to become more formalised and to expand on a global scale. The seed that was to grow into Rokpa was planted by His Holiness the 16th Karmapa and His Eminence Jamgon Kongtrul when, during their visit to Samye Ling in 1977, they met a young Swiss actress called Lea Wyler. Lea was preoccupied with grief at the recent death of her mother and was completely taken aback when Jamgon Kongtrul asked her to start an organisation to help Tibetan refugee monks in the Karmapa's Rumtek Monastery in Sikkim. She was even more astonished to be invited in to His Holiness' apartment where His Holiness dictated a list of the Lamas needing help as Jamgon Kongtrul wrote down their names. When His Holiness handed her the list Lea found herself promising to do what she could to help the Lamas in need.

It was only after His Holiness had left Samye Ling that Lea realised she had no idea how to go about fulfilling her promise. She wrote to Jamgon Kongtrul explaining her difficulty and was much surprised to receive a reply telling her not to worry and that he would help her when she came to Rumtek Monastery. As Lea had barely heard of Rumtek and certainly had no intention of going there she found this rather puzzling. However, two years later, she joined some twenty people who were accompanying Akong Rinpoche on a pilgrimage of the holy sites of India and Nepal. The condition of joining the pilgrimage was that each pilgrim would commit to raising the same amount of money that they would spend on the trip for the purpose of giving offerings at all the holy sites and in this way benefit many beings as well as themselves.

The poverty Lea encountered in India was an eye opener for the erstwhile actress who had never before seen beggars and lepers. On one memorable day in Bodhgaya, where the streets were lined with poor and ailing mendicants, Lea felt she really had to do something for these unfortunate people. She bought a large amount of bread and started handing it out right there on the street. Within minutes she was surrounded by a crowd of people pushing and fighting to get the food. One old woman hit a young child who had grabbed a piece of bread. The bread fell from the child's hand and was promptly snapped up by a starving dog. It became obvious to Lea that she would have to find another way to help.

Later that day she went to the bank and changed some currency for a sack full of coins. Once again she went among the street beggars and tried to distribute the coins fairly, one for each person. This second attempt at charity caused a near riot as people pushed and shoved to get the money. One coin she had meant to give to a blind boy fell onto the street and rolled away to be picked up by someone else. Unaware of this the blind boy began scrabbling in the dust, frantically searching for his coin only to be laughed at by the crowd. Lea was mortified to find her good intentions had caused such a scene.

In the evening of that same day, as she made her way to meet up with friends for dinner, Lea bumped into a leper who sat begging outside the restaurant. As he stretched out his hand towards her their arms touched. She instinctively recoiled in horror then, ashamed of her own reaction, immediately burst into tears. The leper laughed at her and suddenly their roles were reversed. It was this third incident on that fateful day which was a seminal moment for Lea and became a great turning point in her life. Later the pilgrimage continued on to Rumtek Monastery in Sikkim where Lea finally met up with Jamgon Kongtrul and was able to seek his advice on how to raise funds for the impoverished Lamas of the monastery.

Once back in Switzerland, after her life changing trip, Lea decided to relinquish her acting career in favour of working to help those in need. She asked all the wealthy people she knew if they would help but was largely met with puzzlement or unwanted advice to stick to acting. Eventually she managed to persuade a few people to give her some money to sponsor refugee Tibetan monks, although she had the distinct impression they were giving more out of pity for her than for the refugees. When she returned to Samye Ling Lea asked Akong Rinpoche if he would help her with her efforts. At first, perhaps to test her resolve, Rinpoche advised her to just carry on as she was.

A year later, after having continued with her fundraising in Switzerland, Lea returned to Samye Ling. This time Rinpoche agreed to help. Together they settled on naming the charity Rokpa, the Tibetan word meaning help, and Rinpoche immediately sketched his idea for the logo which was then beautifully drawn and painted by Carlo Luyckx. Rinpoche also accompanied Lea to her home in Zurich where he met her father, a well respected lawyer, who agreed to handle the legal side of setting up the charity and its constitution. In 1981 Rokpa International was duly established with Akong Rinpoche as the President and Lea Wyler as vice president. With Akong Rinpoche as the figurehead the charity work moved up a gear. People began to trust that it would really work and started to give money to sponsor the Rumtek monks then many other predominantly Tibetan refugees in India and Nepal.

In 1983 Akong Rinpoche made his first trip back to Tibet since leaving in 1959. Although he encountered much suffering and destruction in his homeland he refused to engage in negative thinking and instead set his mind one pointedly on relieving people's suffering as much as possible. When he returned to the UK Rinpoche brought many photographs of people he had met in great need. Lea added them to the growing list she was already finding sponsorship for and so it was that Rokpa gradually began to grow.

After continuing to help an increasing number of people with these individual sponsorships Lea began to think about how to reach more people with a larger scale project. Akong Rinpoche had been thinking along similar lines and suggested that Rokpa could start a soup kitchen in Nepal which could feed the poor and hungry during the coldest months of the winter. In 1990 Lea arranged to meet Akong Rinpoche in Nepal. Arriving at Rinpoche's hotel in the evening, somewhat jetlagged after her long flight, she was amazed to find out that Rinpoche was scheduled to leave for Tibet the following morning. Consequently most of that night was spent taking notes and receiving instructions from Akong Rinpoche on how to start the Rokpa soup kitchen.

With the help of monks from Thrangu Rinpoche's Monastery Lea set up the soup kitchen near the Great Stupa of Boudnath in Kathmandu. As one of the most sacred Buddhist sites in the world the stupa attracts thousands of pilgrims every day. It also draws many poor and destitute people who come to beg particularly in the harsh Himalayan winter therefore it was an ideal location from which to reach a large number of needy people. The soup kitchen has run every year since then and, having expanded considerably, is nowadays staffed by between twenty to thirty international volunteers.

All in all 1990 was a landmark year for the Rokpa Charity as it saw, not only the setting up of Rokpa's first soup kitchen in Nepal but also the establishment of Rokpa's first projects inside Tibet. During his previous visits to Tibet Akong Rinpoche had encountered many people experiencing great hardship and although he had managed to help many individuals through finding sponsorship he wanted to do something that would help greater numbers of people, preferably in sustainable ways. His first idea was to travel to some of the worst off regions and talk to the people themselves to find out what they thought would be of most benefit. As money was so tight Rinpoche could not afford much in the way of transport and frequently travelled the country in the back of a truck clinging on to whatever came to hand as the vehicle lurched along the rough hewn roads.

Through many meetings with villagers and nomads in some of Tibet's most remote regions Rinpoche began to ascertain what kind of aid would be most beneficial, not only in the short term but with a view to long term projects that could help people help themselves. Broadly speaking these projects fell into the categories of healthcare, education, cultural preservation and environmental protection. Healthcare was one of the most urgent issues as so few people had access to any kind of medical treatment. Therefore Rokpa's first projects were to set up clinics and provide some basic child care and education, particularly for orphan children.

Lea Wyler continued to raise funds for Rokpa projects from her base in Switzerland, but by the early nineties Rokpa started to set up branches in other European countries to help the fundraising effort. First of these was the UK branch based at Samye Ling. Marian Dreyfus was Rokpa's first UK representative and was followed by a succession of other volunteers until 1993 when the present representative Victoria Long took over. Victoria runs the busy Rokpa Office from Samye Ling and is helped by Marilyn Harris and many other unpaid volunteers who contribute their time and skills on a regular basis. Other countries have followed suit and today Rokpa has branches in eighteen countries staffed almost entirely by volunteers. These branches raise funds for poor and needy people in Tibet, Nepal, India and Africa as well as running projects in their own countries fulfilling Rokpa's mission "to help wherever help is needed." A full list of Rokpa branches are listed at the back of this book in Chapter XVII.

Every year representatives from all the Rokpa branches around the world congregate at Samye Ling for the annual Rokpa General meeting hosted by Akong Rinpoche. It is a time to reunite and compare notes with friends and colleagues engaged in Rokpas' many activities. To detail these would require a book in itself, but suffice it to say that in Tibet alone Rokpa now runs a hundred and fifty projects, including schools, colleges, medical colleges, clinics, arts and crafts training, and environmental projects. By working with local authorities as well as the indigenous population Rokpa has become a well respected, highly efficient organisation and a lifeline for countless people offering them help in the present and hope for the future. The increased scope of Rokpa's activity around the world, and particularly in Tibet, has led to greater interest from the media. One particular article written in 1995 by Samye Ling nun, Ani Rinchen Khandro, appeared in the UK magazine Kindred Spirit. The article contained an in depth interview with Akong Rinpoche which told how his life's journey had led to the establishment of Rokpa. The story touched the heart of rock star Annie Lennox who at that time was scheduled to appear in a Charity Concert in Los Angeles. The VH1 Honours Concert was to feature a host of internationally acclaimed recording stars who were being honoured not only for their talent but also their charity work. Each artist was to nominate a charity to receive a share of the Concerts' proceeds. Annie Lennox chose Rokpa.

Akong Rinpoche, Lama Yeshe Losal and Ani Rinchen Khandro then found themselves in the unlikely situation of being flown to the US to attend the Concert, at the appropriately named Shrine Auditorium, along with the rock glitterati of L.A. After meeting Akong Rinpoche, Annie Lennox was so moved and impressed with his work that she graciously donated not only her share of the Concert proceeds but also topped it up with a donation of her own. She has been a firm friend of Samye Ling and Rokpa ever since.

Many other people, well known or not, have been inspired over the years by Rokpa's work around the world. Following Akong Rinpoche's example they have found for themselves that to give unconditionally benefits not only the recipient but also the person giving. Not everyone is in a position to give money, but one can always give kindness, skills, labour, or that precious commodity, time. Everyone has something to give and can follow Rokpa's motto 'Helping Where Help is Needed.'

Lea Wyler, Akong Rinpoche and Dr. Veit Wyler

Akong Rinpoche and Rokpa projects in Tibet

Rokpa Children's Home

Lea Wyler and Rokpa projects in Nepal

Rokpa Soup Kitchen

H.E. Tai Situpa, Akong Rinpoche and Rokpa workers

Annie Lennox and Lama Yeshe Losal

Completion of the long retreat

CHAPTER X

RITES OF PASSAGE

As a result of the proliferation of Rokpa's work Akong Rinpoche found himself increasingly absent from Samye Ling. Much of his time became devoted to travelling to Tibet and many other parts of the world to oversee a growing number of projects and set up new ones. As spiritual director of the Samye Dzong Centres, which were becoming established in various countries, Akong Rinpoche was also committed to visit them and give teachings and advice on a yearly basis where possible. Like a conjuror spinning plates Rinpoche travelled the globe injecting each of his projects with a charge of energy and guiding their progress with his boundless wisdom and compassion.

On one memorable trip to Tibet in 1992 Rinpoche received some long awaited news concerning the reincarnation of His Holiness Karmapa. Akong Rinpoche was given directions to the whereabouts of the young child and asked to verify whether he was indeed the Karmapa. On reaching the particular nomad's tent in a valley of Kham the family of the young boy welcomed Akong Rinpoche. Another party of monks had already arrived and after testing the boy seemed satisfied that the lively seven year old was indeed the Karmapa. Akong Rinpoche had his own personal test to conduct.

When the previous Karmapa had fallen ill Akong Rinpoche had been at his bedside in the hospital in America. His Holiness knew he was soon to die and was making practical arrangements with some of his closest disciples. During that time Akong Rinpoche asked His Holiness if he would leave him one of his teeth as a holy relic. This might seem like rather a strange request but in Tibetan Buddhism it is not uncommon to keep a personal fragment of a holy being as an object of great veneration. The Karmapa at once agreed. However, just before His Holiness passed away he sent Akong Rinpoche on a mission, which meant that he was absent when the funeral rites were conducted and consequently was not given His Holiness' tooth.

Twelve years later, on entering the nomad's tent in Kham, Akong Rinpoche went up to the rosy cheeked boy and asked if he had anything to give him. The boy unhesitatingly reached under the rug he was sitting on and pulled something out. He then proffered his open hand to Rinpoche and there, sitting in the middle of his palm, was a tiny milk tooth. Rinpoche was overjoyed and gathered His Holiness up in his arms. The Karmapa was not at all fazed by the turn of events but grinned and ruffled Rinpoche's hair as if greeting a long lost friend.

The Karmapa was then taken to his monastery at Tsurphu and after receiving an official letter of recognition from His Holiness the Dalai Lama and the formal recognition of the Kagyu Lineage Regents as well as that of the Chinese Government, His Holiness was enthroned in September 1992 in an elaborate ceremony presided over by His Eminence Tai Situpa. Tens of thousands of Tibetans were joined by disciples from all over the world who flocked to attend the enthronement, including Akong Rinpoche, Lama Yeshe Losal, Sherab Palden and some twenty fortunate devotees from Samye Ling. Although only seven, His Holiness sat composed throughout the long and impressive ceremony then gave blessings to the vast throng of people who filed past his throne. When Lama Yeshe Losal presented his offering to the young Karmapa and asked if he might be allowed to go back into retreat His Holiness 'blessed' Lama Yeshe with a swift kick to the head and the instruction, " Go back and help your brother!"

Back at Samye Ling the second long retreat finished and the retreatants were ceremoniously led in a proccession to the temple by Lama Yeshe where Akong Rinpoche welcomed them with words of wisdom before they were reunited with their friends and families. Akong Rinpoche also told the Samye Ling community of all the amazing circumstances leading up to the enthronement of His Holiness the 17th Gyalwa Karmapa Orgyen Trinley Dorje. As head of the Kagyu Lineage His Holiness is the pinnacle and focal point for all Kagyu Monasteries and practitioners therefore the news of his discovery and subsequent enthronement was greeted with great joy at Kagyu Centres around the world. Although His Holiness was still a young boy the Samye Ling community could now look forward to him one day visiting his seat in Scotland as his much loved predecessor had done. In the meantime Samye Ling had another very important visitor to prepare for.

His Holiness the Dalai Lama was invited to visit Samye Ling during his tour of the UK in 1993. In preparation for his visit the community came together to build a spacious Conference Centre annexed to Fir Tree Lodge situated behind the temple. Mel Du Pontet was one of the principal builders and spent days, ankle deep in mud while brick laying the new building. The interior, with its pyramid like wooden ceiling, was largely created by Andrew Gordon while Vin Harris fitted the doors and windows. However, the whole community worked together to complete the building in time to receive their illustrious visitor.

In May 1993 His Holiness the Dalai Lama made his second visit to Samye Ling. Although it was almost summer the weather was unseasonably cold and six inches of snow fell the day before his arrival. Thousands of people converged on Samye Ling to greet His Holiness, who laughed good naturedly at the weather and said the snow made him feel as if he was at home in Tibet. When His Holiness first visited Samye Ling in 1984 he had given teachings in the newly built Samye Ling temple, which was just a shell of a building with unfinished walls. Since then the temple interior had long been completed and magnificently decorated. When His Holiness entered the shrine room to address the residents and guests he was visibly impressed by the huge change since his last visit and by Akong Rinpoche's response that "It was done by the community".

Even the great shrine room could not accommodate the thousands of people who gathered to hear His Holiness' public talk. Consequently a huge marquee had been erected in front of the temple where some three and a half thousand people sat spellbound as the great Boddhisattva spoke with such wisdom, compassion and utter humility that many were moved to tears. The Dalai Lama spent three days at Samye Ling, giving teachings, attending pujas and inspiring everyone with his joyful presence. He also unveiled a plaque, together with Lord David Steel, to commemorate the building of the first stage of Samye Phase II.

Meanwhile in Tibet, the presence of the young Karmapa at his Monastery in Tsurphu, together with the increasing number of Rokpa projects, gave Akong Rinpoche more reason than ever to make protracted visits to his homeland. His commitment to visit Samye Ling's other branches around the world also added to his peripatetic lifestyle and meant that he was frequently away from Samye Ling for months on end. In order to fill the gap created by his absence Rinpoche asked his brother, Lama Yeshe Losal, to become more involved in the day to day running of Samye Ling.

Although Lama Yeshe's previous experience of setting up and running the Karma Triyana Dharmachakra Centre in New York made him the ideal candidate to take over the management of Samye Ling, his own wish was to continue meditating in strict solitary retreat. Apart from a short break to meet his visiting brother and sister, Lama Yeshe had been in retreat since 1980. He had become Retreat Master to the western Buddhists practitioners at Purelands Retreat Centre, but when they left at the end of their retreat Lama Yeshe stayed on in solitary seclusion. However, in 1990, while still acting as Retreat Master for the second long retreat, Lama Yeshe acceded to his brother's request and began to divide his time between his fulfilling his duties at Purelands and taking on new responsibilities at Samye Ling.

By this time the Samye temple was fully functioning, not only as a shrine room but also as a nucleus for the Centre's activities, providing the ideal space for holding a variety of courses and weekend workshops in such subjects as meditation, yoga, tai chi and various Rokpa Therapy courses. The wide range of activities on offer drew large numbers of people from a broad spectrum of society. Buddhism and alternative therapies had become more main stream and Samye Ling was attracting more and more media attention as a place to learn about such things or simply to come and relax away from the pressures of modern life.

Very often people would arrive at Samye Ling, attend a weekend course and then wish to stay and become part of the community. Many were young people with problems of one kind or another that they were seeking to solve. Invariably they would ask for an interview with Lama Yeshe Losal to request his help. As well as having the spiritual wisdom which was the fruit of many years meditation practice Lama Yeshe also had first hand understanding of the problems facing people in modern life, having had experience of them in his youth. His relaxed, informal manner and non judgemental attitude also made it easy for people to open their hearts and express themselves to him.

Lama Yeshe was not officially recognised as a tulku, nor was he a doctor or a therapist like Akong Rinpoche, but a monk and meditator who had overcome his own difficulties through diligently practising the dharma. Meditation was his medicine and he had no hesitation in recommending it to others as a way out of their problems. He could also see that people who were leading unhealthy life styles may not have the will or discipline to apply the remedy. Knowing how much he had been helped by taking vows as a monk he determined to find a way that others could follow a similar path.

In Tibetan culture it is quite normal to take ordination for life but things were different in the West and Lama Yeshe knew people would be unlikely to make such a long term commitment. His solution was to allow people to take a beginner's ordination for one year then to carry on for a further two or three years or to give back their robes if they wished. There was no precedent in Tibetan Buddhism for the giving of one year ordination so Lama Yeshe first had to seek permission from the acting head of the Kagyu Lineage, His Eminence Tai Situpa. Once Tai Situpa had given his blessing for the initiative Lama Yeshe was able to give one year ordination to a number of young men and women who came to live at Samye Ling as monks and nuns observing the eight root vows.

The proliferation of ordained sangha, with their shaven heads and flowing burgundy robes soon became a commonplace sight at Samye Ling as the new monks and nuns joined the lay residents to become part of the community. Although the sangha had to study Buddhist teachings and attend pujas they were also expected to muck in with the multitude of jobs involved in running the Centre. As with any new initiative there were occasional teething problems. Sometimes visitors to Samye Ling would assume that a monk or nun would be well versed in Buddhism and able to give advice whereas in fact they may have only just got ordained and know very little, while a lay person in ordinary clothes might be a very experienced practitioner. Therefore Lama Yeshe advised the sangha to be very honest in their dealings with visitors and to direct them to experienced teachers rather than try to answer questions themselves. He also clarified the various levels of vows and the behaviour appropriate for members of the sangha as set out in guidelines issued to everyone taking ordination.

By and large the ordination of sangha has been a great success and has given hundreds of people the opportunity to get their lives back on track. Strengthened by the experience some people would leave after their year was up and go on to lead more meaningful lives in society. Others would choose to renew their vows and deepen their practice of the Dharma for a few more years while still others would gain such benefit from the experience that they would happily commit themselves to taking life long vows.

Having been able to experience life as a monk or nun in a gradual way many sangha have found that in giving up worldly life they have actually gained more freedom and happiness as a result. Some of the life ordained monks and nuns continue to live at Samye Ling where many of them study, work and pass on the teachings of Buddhadharma to people both inside and outside the community, while others have left to perform similar functions at various Samye Dzong Centres around the UK and in different parts of the world.

There are three levels of ordination within the Tibetan tradition, these being Genyin which is the beginner's level, Getsul which is novitiate level, and Gelong which is full ordination. At Samye Ling a person would usually take the Genyin vows for one or two years then progress to the Getsul vows for anything from three years up to life long ordination. Monks could also take further vows of full Gelong ordination but that option was not open to nuns as the Gelongma tradition had not survived as an unbroken lineage in Tibet.

In 1998 an unprecedented opportunity arose to re-establish the Gelongma ordination for nuns within the Tibetan Buddhist tradition. A full ordination ceremony for both monks and nuns was being held at the sacred place of Bodhgaya. This historic ceremony had the backing of all the major Buddhist traditions and was to be presided over by the Chinese Venerable Master Hsing Yun, founder of the Fokuangshan Buddhist Order of Taiwan, with the involvement of twenty seven fully ordained monks and twelve fully ordained nuns as witnesses. As the full ordination of nuns had survived in the Chinese Lineage it would thus be possible to ordain nuns from other Buddhist lineages who wished to take full ordination.

As Abbot of the main Tibetan Buddhist monastery in Europe, Lama Yeshe Losal had been invited to act as one of the preceptors of the ceremony. It would be the first time that a Tibetan Lama would participate in a ceremony that was to see the full ordination of over a hundred nuns and some twenty monks. It was also a unique opportunity for those life ordained nuns at Samye Ling who wanted to take Gelongma vows. Lama Yeshe also wished to honour the occasion by making the journey to Bodhgaya part of a pilgrimage to visit the main holy sites of the Lord Buddha and on February 11th 1998 Lama Yeshe Losal, accompanied by eleven nuns, boarded the plane to Delhi to start the first leg of their pilgrimage.

After a few days of rest and acclimatisation in Delhi the group took the train to Bodhgaya where they had a day to visit the ancient holy sites of Vulture Peak and Nalanda University before starting the preparations and training for the ordination. These were to start on February 15th and go on until the beginning of the ordination ceremony itself on February 20th. However, just as everything had been going to plan a completely unforeseen occurrence took place on the morning of February 19th.

Just before the morning training session was due to begin some of the Samye Ling nuns joined a group of Ladakhi nuns who were holding a Tara Puja underneath the sacred Bodhi tree. Amongst them was Ani Chopel, a Spanish nun who had done many years of retreat at Purelands and on Holy Island. Although Ani Chopel had a long standing heart condition she had been given the go ahead to travel to India by her doctor and had indeed coped well with the rigours of the journey. However, there under the tree where the Buddha became enlightened Ani Chopel suddenly fainted. Lama Yeshe sat with her waiting for the ambulance but before it could get there Ani Chopel passed away peacefully under the Bodhi tree, with her Lama and dharma sisters by her side at one of the world's holiest Buddhist sites.

Of course it was extremely shocking for her family and everyone who knew her, but once the news had sunk in people began to see the positive side of the extraordinary occurrence. Given that death is inevitable for all beings, Buddhists consider it extremely auspicious to die in a holy place and the remarkable circumstances of Ani Chopel's death were considered by her teachers, her dharma sisters and everyone attending the historic ceremony in Bodhgaya as being truly blessed.

The following day, as the nun's ordination ceremony began, Ani Chopel was in the thoughts of everyone there, not only the people from Samye Ling, and although her body was not present she was very much there in spirit. The ceremony continued throughout the night then, after a few hours rest, recommenced the next morning as the nuns were joined by the monks. At the conclusion of the elaborate ceremony the elated, newly ordained sangha emerged from the temple to receive congratulations from crowds of well wishers outside.

Lama Yeshe Losal and the Samye Ling nuns then went to attend Ani Chopel's cremation. A large crowd of monks, nuns and lay devotees of many denominations had also gathered, many of whom had been sponsored to come and pray. Chopel's body was gently placed in a special box in a truck and covered with mounds of flower garlands, incense and candles. A long convoy of vehicles slowly followed the truck, with hundreds of people walking alongside until they reached the cremation site where a pyre had been prepared on the bank of the river Neranjara.

Ani Chopel's sister, who is the Spanish Commissioner in the European Parliament flew in from Spain with her partener who is the Greek High Commisioner, to attend the cremation. Lama Yeshe and Chopel's sister lit the funeral pyre together. With the rising of the flames a fragrant scent of incense filled the air. The Tibetan monks chanted, the Samye Ling nuns prayed and Lama Yeshe Losal stood quietly by the fire then finally threw a katta on the flames. As the fire died down the sun's rays burst through a cloud directly above the pyre, as if the Buddha's light itself had shone down to welcome Chopel.

As Lama Yeshe later recalled, "Ani Chopel passed away under the most auspicious circumstances possible. As far as we know it is the first time anyone has ever died under the sacred Bodhi tree at the place where the Buddha became enlightened. Her funeral brought togehter all the different Buddhist groups and I remember Chopel's sister saying that the moment we lit the pyre all sadness was lifted from her and she felt an overwhelming sense of peace and happiness".

In the days that followed the newly ordained Gelongmas took their Bodhisattva vows alongside the Gelongs then left Bodhgaya to complete their pilgrimage to the holy sites of Sarnath, where the Lord Buddha first taught, then to Kushnigar where he died and attained Parinirvana and on to Lumbini where he was born. The group then flew to Nepal where they were delighted to meet up with Akong Rinpoche and members of his family. The next few days were spent partly helping Rinpoche and Lea Wyler with the Rokpa soup kitchen and partly visiting stupas, monasteries, ancient meditation caves and other sacred places in and around Kathmandu.

The group then flew back to Delhi and boarded a bus for the long journey to Tai Situpa's Sherab Ling Monastery where they spent a week visiting yet more holy sites, principally the caves and Lake of Tso Pema where Guru Rinpoche meditated and performed many miracles. On the final leg of their journey Lama Yeshe and the nuns travelled back to Delhi for a few days rest before boarding a plane to the UK, thus completing the full circle of their eventful pilgrimage.

Later that year Lama Yeshe made another important journey, travelling to Sri Lanka to attend the Award Ceremony of the Sarvodaya Bikkhu Congress where he was awarded the title of Sasana Kirti Sri, or Illustrious Renowned Teacher. This historic occasion demonstrated the esteem in which Lama Yeshe is held by the different schools of Buddhism as he became the first Tibetan Buddhist Lama to be honoured by the Theravadin tradition in this significant and ground breaking way. During that same trip Lama Yeshe, accompanied by a monk and nun from Samye Ling, was taken on pilgrimage to the main Buddhist Holy places in Sri Lanka, including the sacred site where the holy relic of the Buddha's tooth is kept. The pilgrimage continued with a tour of the Buddhist sites in Burma, taking in the opening of the first Buddhist College, and concluded with a tour of sacred places in Thailand. In this way Lama Yeshe Losal reinforced links and demonstrated his wish to work in harmony with all three schools of Buddhism.

His Holiness the 17th Karmapa and Akong Rinpoche

H.H. the 17th Karmapa

H.E. Khentin Tai Situpa

Kenchen Thrangu Rinpoche

Ringu Tulku Rinpoche

H.H. Dalai Lama and Lord David Steele at the inauguration of Samye Project Phase 2

Akong Rinpoche and H.H. Dalai Lama

H.E. Tai Situpa and the Mahamudra group

Lama Yeshe Losal at the Sarvidaya Bikkhu Congress in Sri Lanka

Bikkhuni Ordination at Bodhgaya

CHAPTER XI

ISLAND OF DREAMS

Soon after Lama Yeshe Losal took over the day to day running of Samye Ling he received a visit from a Mrs. Kay Morris. It transpired that Mrs. Morris was the owner of a small island off the west coast of Scotland which, due to family circumstances, she wished to sell. Mrs. Morris explained that she was a Catholic and had had a very powerful dream in which Mary Mother of Christ had appeared to her and said that she should offer her island to the Buddhist community of Samye Ling. Lama Yeshe replied that it was a lovely idea but that he was a monk, who had only just come out of twelve years of retreat and he had no money to buy a house let alone an island. However, Mrs Morris insisted that Lama Yeshe should at least come and see the island for himself, and so, partly because he did not wish to offend and partly because he was intrigued, Lama Yeshe agreed to go.

On a crisp winter's morning in December 1990 Lama Yeshe, accompanied by a couple of Samye Ling residents and Mrs. Morris's son sailed from the Isle of Arran to the small but impressive Holy Isle and first set eyes on its wild beauty crowned by the imposing peak of Mullach Mor wreathed in mist. Once ashore Lama Yeshe felt an immediate affinity for the island's rugged terrain, so reminiscent of his lost homeland of Tibet. He explored the island with all the agility of its resident mountain goats, climbing to the top with such speed that his companions, David Cameron and Maria Martinelli were hard pushed to keep up. Maria even succumbed to a nose bleed through the exertion!

As the light began to fade Mr. Morris said they would have to leave the island before the nightfall. However, Lama Yeshe who had started to feel a strong connection to the place said he wished to stay the night. Mr. Morris said that was not possible as there was nowhere suitable for them to sleep, but Lama Yeshe was not to be deterred. He sat on the pebble beach gazing out to sea as the grey dusk turned into an ink blue night and the coast of Arran across the bay started to twinkle with street lights illuminating its sinuous shoreline. The magical panorama before him suddenly awoke a long forgotten memory with deep and irresistible force.

Many years before, when still on retreat in America Lama Yeshe had experienced a very vivid dream during his practice of dream yoga. He dreamt he was flying over a beautiful island in semi darkness. The nearby coastline was lit up with what he thought must be thousands of butterlamp offerings. The dream was so realistic that Lama Yeshe asked his teacher what it could mean. However, Khenpo Karthar wisely told him not to dwell on it as it would only disturb his practice and any significance it might have would emerge in its own good time.

At the recollection of his dream Lama Yeshe knew with unshakeable certainty that his fate and that of the Holy Island were inextricably entwined and that he should do everything in his power to acquire it. Having found out about the island's ancient history as a place of great spiritual significance in pre Christian and Celtic Christian times Lama Yeshe felt inspired by a vision to reawaken its sacred past and to make it a place of refuge and retreat, not only for Buddhists but for people of all faiths.

In Celtic times the island was known as Inis Shroin, or Isle of the Water Spirits. In the 6th century a young prince named Laisren gave up his rights to the throne of Ulster to pursue a spiritual life and chose to live as a hermit in a cave on Holy Island. Although Laisren meditated in solitude, news of his wisdom and miraculous powers soon spread and many people made the trip to Holy Island to seek out the holy man and ask his advice. After his death Laisren was sanctified and became known as Saint Molaise. His cave became a place of pilgrimage, as did the nearby spring whose holy waters are reputed to have healing properties. There are obvious parallels between Saint Molaise's life and that of the Buddha, who also gave up a kingdom to pursue spiritual life. Indeed, in Tibetan Buddhism it is not uncommon for yogis, such as the great Tibetan Saints Guru Rinpoche and Milarepa, to forsake worldly life and spend many years meditating in caves. Lama Yeshe felt inspired by the spiritual legacy of Holy Island and so determined to reawaken it as a sacred, healing place for our times.

On return to Samye Ling Lama Yeshe told Akong Rinpoche of his wish to acquire Holy Island and of his plan to develop it as a Retreat Centre and a place of spiritual and environmental sanctity which would benefit all beings. Akong Rinpoche was immediately supportive and said he would do what he could to help, but knowing how busy he was Lama Yeshe told his brother that he only required his blessing and that he would raise the funds himself. Lama Yeshe's enthusiasm for his project was infectious and before long he gathered around him a team of Samye Ling residents who became inspired by his vision of Holy Island. A prominent member of the Holy Island Project team was Thom McCarthy, an American Samye Ling resident with considerable business acumen. Lama Yeshe's vision, coupled with Thom's drive, Claudine Maurois help and the team's hard work and dedication became a formidable fundraising machine.

So intent was Kay Morris that the island should go to the Buddhists that she refused higher offers from other parties and dropped her asking price to put the island within reach. After a massive fundraising effort Holy Island was finally signed over to the Rokpa Trust in April 1992. Media interest was colossal. The island seemed to catch the imagination of people around the world. Volunteer workers started to arrive and begin the island's environmental clean up operation, rubbing shoulders with press and TV crews keen to cover the story. Monks, nuns and lay people of many nationalities camped out in tents as Lama Yeshe directed the work. Acquiring the island was one thing but there was a tremendous amount of work to be done to make it habitable. Raising funds and awareness of the Holy Island Project was an ongoing job for the team but gradually the hard work began to pay off as people donated funds or their labour on a regular basis.

The light house cottages at the south end of the island were the first buildings to be renovated and by 1993 one of them was not only habitable but actually warm and comfortable. Lama Yeshe had earmarked the upstairs of the house for visiting Lamas, while residents occupied the downstairs rooms. Alex Duncan was caretaker and took charge of the volunteer workers in Lama Yeshe's absence. The old boiler room of the lighthouse was converted into a makeshift shrine room so that the handful of resident workers could keep up with their spiritual practice. Meanwhile, at the north end of the island the semi derelict old farmhouse was cleaned up and used as a squat for volunteers to use if the weather was too rough for camping. There was also a small annexe which was dry and habitable enough for a group of resident workers. During the summer months visitors would camp out and help with volunteer work such as dry stone walling, tree planting, light building work and a host of other tasks. Although facilities were rough and ready there was a cheerful pioneering spirit that prevailed and the wild beauty of Holy Island with its sacred cave of Saint Molaise, its holy well, and abundant wild life more than made up for the lack of mod cons.

The island had no trouble in attracting volunteers, and fortunately these always seemed to include wonderful cooks so there were always masses of hearty vegetarian meals to sustain the workers. Workshop leaders were also drawn to the island and ran a variety of popular courses such as meditation, tai chi and yoga which volunteers could attend for a few hours a day alternating with periods of environmental work. The camaraderie that built up between people working together to accomplish a common goal was a very special experience for all concerned and inspired many people to return year after year to devote their time and energy to the Holy Island Project.

As Lama Yeshe's plan for the island began to take shape, he decided that the South end would eventually take over from the Purelands Retreat as a place for committed practitioners to take part in long term cloistered retreats. The North end of the island would become an interfaith Centre where people of all faiths or none could participate in courses, gatherings, or short retreats that would enhance peace, health and understanding. Plans were drawn up to renovate the old farmhouse and make it the central part of a U shaped building that would respect the existing traditional architecture while providing two accommodation wings with all amenities. A courtyard would be formed by the addition of another building at the back which would be the Peace Hall where courses and conferences would take place.

Lama Yeshe delighted in showing visitors around the island, not least the Tibetan Buddhist Lamas who were drawn to its familiarly rugged landscape of hills, caves, green paths instead of roads and the abundant wildlife. Ancient breeds of Soay sheep and Sanaan goats shared the slopes and plains with a herd of wild Eriskay ponies, living in harmony in a wholly natural environment. His Eminence Tai Situpa was an early visitor and, after exploring the island, used his knowledge of geomancy to help Lama Yeshe choose the best location for the long Retreat Centre. The Holy Island Project then launched an international Architectural Competition attracting sixty entries from architects around the world who submitted designs for the Retreat. Part of their remit was to design buildings that would harmonise with the island's terrain and be sensitive to its ecology. The competition garnered more media coverage for Holy Island, especially when Scottish comedian Billy Connolly kindly presented prizes at the award ceremony in Glasgow's Saint Mungo's Museum. As someone who had also expressed interest in buying Holy Island, Billy Connolly joked that the Buddhists had beaten him to it.

The design which answered the brief most fittingly was by Andrew Wright, a young architect who had been a protégé of Sir Richard Rogers. His series of terraced meditation cells built in to the contours of the hill was a wonderfully organic design which would make minimal impact on the environment. However, as an extremely innovative idea it would take much time, expense and effort to make it a reality. In the meantime Lama Yeshe felt that the first building priority should be at the north end as that would become the Centre for World Peace and Health which would have a wider application than the long term retreat since it would be used by people of all faiths and backgrounds.

At the Holy Island office set up in Samye Ling, Nick Jennings took over the fundraising job after Thom McCarthy moved on, working closely with engineer David Cameron, Lama Yeshe's secretary Ani Lhamo and the rest of the Project team to apply for funding for buildings and environmental work. Grants for tree planting were given and, combined with tree sponsorship from private individuals, have helped to reforest the island with a variety of native tree species. Forrester Ken Mills guided the tree planting project while resident monk Rinchen worked with countless volunteers over the years to not only plant some 35,000 indigenous trees but also fence off the sapling plantations to prevent them from being eaten by wild animals. Large areas of bracken, brambles and rhododendron were cleared to provide extra grazing for the wild ponies, goats and sheep. In this way the animals, who also supplement their diet with nutritious seaweed, have thrived and their numbers increased. Lama Yeshe's policy has always been to maintain a healthy balance between the needs of flora and fauna so that all forms of island life can flourish in harmony.

In 1997 Ani Rinchen Khandro, a nun with previous media experience took over the fundraising, publicity, and course programme production for both Samye Ling and Holy Island. Having already lead tai chi courses on Holy Island for the volunteers she was well acquainted with the island and its residents with whom she kept in close contact from the Holy Island Office base at Samye Ling. The island's resident building team, led by Malcom Wylie, ably abetted by Zangpo, Chenden, Kunley, Namdrol, Leo, Joe and many seasonal volunteers, made great progress with gutting the farmhouse before starting on the major renovation work. Funds raised from Trusts and thousands of individual supporters were channelled to the island to pay for building materials. Throughout the busy summers and the quiet winters in still very basic living conditions, the builders and seasonal volunteers were sustained by the delicious meals produced in a rather primitive kitchen by a succession of volunteer cooks who deserve much credit for the wonderful food and the homely atmosphere they managed to create despite the difficult circumstances.

During this time another project was underway at Samye Ling to build a traditional Mongolian style tent, or yurt, for use on Holy Island as a temporary space in which to hold meetings and meditation sessions. Thanks to yurt maker Hal Wynne Jones and his students Phurbu, Rabje, Melong and Mark, a beautiful yurt was made and erected in the summer of '98 when it was inaugurated by Lama Yeshe Losal at the start of the first interfaith gathering to be held on Holy Island. The yurt was used from then on for annual interfaith meetings, courses and as a place of prayer and meditation for residents and guests.

As well as the continuing building and environmental work, Holy Island also experienced a blossoming of artistic expression. The holy cave of Saint Molaise was cleaned and its dirt floor covered with simple stone slabs but it was not changed or decorated in any other way as Lama Yeshe wished to respect it as a place of pilgrimage sacred to all and particularly those of the Christian faith. However, in Tibet it is usual for holy places to be embellished with sacred images so several large rocks and boulders along Holy Island's coastal path were chosen to provide the perfect surface for such inspiring art. The venerable Gyamtso put his stone carving skills to good use and, following Sherab Palden's blueprint, sensitively chiselled the forms of the Buddha and the Kagyu Lineage of Marpa, Milarepa, Gampopa and Dusum Chenpa and more recently White Tara and Green Tara. The rock carvings were later painted, mainly by Dechi and Senge, who produced the colourful images we see today.

The first entirely new building to be erected on Holy Island was thanks to the generosity of an anonymous benefactor, who wished to sponsor a place of retreat for Lama Yeshe. A beautiful wood cabin was built on the South side of the island, nestling into the sheltered lee of the hill. The house was intended for retreat use and had a specially designed dark room where Lama Yeshe could practice the forty nine day Bardo retreat which takes place in complete darkness. However, the cabin's first occupant was Tai Situpa who visited the island in the summer of '96 and formally blessed the house then stayed in it and practiced there, thus consecrating it with his illustrious presence. In 1997 Lama Yeshe closed the doors of the house as he entered a strict period of Bardo Retreat.

Having already done one such retreat in Nepal, Lama Yeshe became one of very few people in the world to successfully accomplish this difficult retreat twice. Because the retreat is conducted in total solitude and complete darkness it requires a very stable mind otherwise one could go insane, but for the rare individuals who are able to withstand the difficulties and privations the forty nine day retreat can bring immense benefit and is the equivalent of spending three year in retreat. By undergoing this most intensive practice on Holy Island Lama Yeshe had not only advanced his own personal journey but had also given tremendous impetus to his aim of reawakening the island's long dormant spiritual heritage.

Around this time another property was unexpectedly acquired by the Holy Island Project. Glenscorrodale Farm on the Isle of Arran had belonged to a young couple who were very supportive of the Project and would happily allow Holy Island volunteers to stay at their farmhouse if bad weather prevented them getting over to the island. Unfortunately Paul Watson, who was suffering from cancer, suddenly took a turn for the worse and died at the age of thirty six. He generously bequeathed the Glenscorrodale Farmhouse to the Holy Island Project in his will. Once the property had changed hands Lama Yeshe sent some of his monks to live there and start to renovate the building. Initially the farmhouse was used as a kind of Holy Island annexe, but in the years to come it would evolve into an important place in its own right, as a twenty two bedroom Men's Retreat which Lama Yeshe dedicated to the memory of Paul Watson.

As Lama Yeshe's vision for Holy Island started to become a reality the Project's high profile continued to attract publicity from major newspapers and television channels in the UK and other countries. The island was also officially designated as a UK Sacred Site by the World Wildlife Fund and Alliance of Religion and Conservation. Some of the raised awareness translated into funding and with the input of a major donation from an anonymous Trust, together with many smaller individual donations, the farmhouse at the North end of the island was beautifully renovated to an extremely high standard. The house could then provide accommodation for up to ten people as well as modern bathroom facilities, a small shrine room and an elegant library.

The standard of workmanship from the volunteer builders was remarkable and boasted such details as an exquisite stained glass window made by craftswoman Ani Chonyi and an intricately carved Kalachakra stone by Melong the stonemason. The additional accommodation meant that, for the first time, visitors to the north end had a choice of camping or opting to stay in the lovingly refurbished farmhouse with the comfort of all modern amenities. Holy Island was growing up. The completed farmhouse was also the vital first stage in the design for the planned Holy Island Centre for World Peace and Health.

Lama Yeshe's first trip to Holy Island

Sanaan goats

Soay sheep

Lama Yeshe with the wild Eriskay ponies

H.R.H. Prince of Wales discussing the Holy Island Project

*Billy Connolly presenting awards at the
Holy Island Architectual Competition*

Lama Yeshe shows rock painting of Marpa to Marie Helvin

Taking the holy waters at Saint Molaise's spring

White Tara rock painting

Garden at the south end

Building the jetty

Holy Island tree plantation

The refurbished Farmhouse

Tibetan centre wedding bridges vastly different cultures

Akong Rinpoche shakes hands with the groom after having given the wedding blessing to his daughter Kami Tarap and Alan Cosgrove on the occasion of their marriage

Photo by Vicki Couchman

Family friend Judge John Maxwell performs the legal wedding ceremony in Samye Ling temple

94

CHAPTER XII

CREATION

After completing his dark retreat Lama Yeshe took up his duties with renewed vigour, running Samye Ling and Holy Island and travelling to many parts of the world to give teachings. His renown as a meditator and charismatic speaker whose direct and down to earth manner gives him the ability to illuminate profound teachings with humour and insight made him much in demand. His increasingly busy schedule took him not only to Dharma Centres but also to events such as the Shell Company Conference in Maastricht where he spoke to an audience of Shell's top six hundred directors and, much to the amazement of their CEO, even got them to meditate.

Meanwhile, at home, more and more people were coming to Samye Ling and although they had a wonderful temple at their disposal the accommodation side of things was distinctly inadequate. Consequently a new accommodation block of some thirty single rooms was built by a mixture of professional builders and volunteer labour. The completion of Potala House meant that many more visitors would be able to attend teachings and courses at Samye Ling and could be housed in comfortable rooms with modern facilities. Improvements and extentions to the existing cafe resulted in the colourful Tibetan Tea Rooms, another innovation that proved popular with residents and visitors alike. Decorated in vibrant colours with traditional Tibetan rugs covering the cushioned seating, the café with its large range of teas and tasty snacks has also became a welcome port of call for many day visitors. The Samye Ling shop was also extended, refitted and stocked with a tempting array of Dharma accoutrements, books, texts and many gift items. The next challenge was to provide the many guests at Samye Ling with a decent dining room.

In the busy summer months everyone would queue along the corridors of Johnstone House, with the long line of people snaking its way upstairs and back again along the passageways before finally reaching the dining room. Then, if the weather was good people would take their food outside and eat in the garden. But in the winter this was not an option, so once the modest dining room was full, guests had to find a seat in the library, on the stairs or wherever they could find a corner. Something had to be done.

An energetic fundraising campaign was begun in order to build the south wing of Phase II. The ground floor of the wing was planned as a new kitchen and food storage area adjacent to an extensive dining hall, capable of seating over two hundred people. The upstairs would consist of a self contained apartment for visiting Lamas and other important personages, the Abbot's office and audience room and accommodation for resident, long term monks. Gradually sufficient funds were raised to start the ambitious building project. Owing to the size of the building work engineer David Cameron worked with professional builders to get the project off the ground, which proceeded in fits and starts, as and when funds were forthcoming.

Ever since His Holiness Dusum Chenpa, the first Karmapa, built numerous large monasteries in Tibet in the 11th century, the Karma Kagyu Lineage established a reputation for being prolific builders. Akong Rinpoche and Lama Yeshe Losal have certainly followed in this tradition and barely has one building project finished than another one begins. The building process, and indeed all work, is seen as part of the participant's development and proceeds according to the individual characters and abilities of those involved. Consequently Samye Ling and Holy Island are constantly developing in an organic way to accommodate the needs of those people helping to create them and of the ever growing number of people wishing to benefit from the spiritual and therapeutic activities they offer.

David Hayward played a major role in the construction of Phase II and worked with his team of men to get the huge skeleton of girders erected. This was of necessity a noisy job and its close proximity to the shrine room meant that people attending prayer and meditation sessions had to get used to the sound of heavy machinery and builders yelling instructions to each other. The resident community soon became inured to the throb of machines and the sometimes colourful language, but some of the guests during that time must have been rather bemused to find tranquillity of their weekend meditation courses set to the 'music' of a building site.

While work was underway on Phase II several smaller but important projects were undertaken by Samye Ling's volunteers. A traditional style Mahakala shrine house was built adjacent to the north side of the main shrine room. Using natural stone slabs the volunteer builders, principally Choga, Chochi and Steve Kent constructed an appropriately rustic building to house a simple yet impressive shrine for the main protector of the Karma Kagyu Lineage. In 1996 Tai Situpa blessed the building, since which time it has been occupied by Ani Dechi who practices Mahakala on a daily basis, often in strict retreat.

Soon after, another project began to build a similarly rustic building along the driveway at the entrance to Samye Ling. This was to be the butter lamp house where up to 1008 butter lamps could be lit as offerings. Chenden, a monk with architectural training, was in charge of the construction which he had designed as a very earthy building, again using natural stone, with a clever ventilation system to channel the smoke and heat of the butter lamps away through vents in the walls. Niches inside the building would be decorated with carved stone panels depicting the Buddha and other holy beings, and the roof was to be covered with copper, which would give a warm glow to the exterior. Chenden and his team of helpers worked hard throughout the year as the building started to take shape.

Meanwhile, long term resident Marion Dreyfus was busy raising funds and awareness for the Stupa Project. Stupas are beautiful monuments representing the Buddha's enlightened mind. Their elegant forms are commonly seen in Tibet and other Buddhist countries where they are revered as sacred structures which radiate positive energy for the benefit of all beings. Building a stupa had always been Akong Rinpoche's intention, particularly since he had discussed the idea with His Holiness the Dalai Lama who suggested it might be part of a Peace Garden at Samye Ling. Then in the late nineties His Eminence Tai Situpa proposed a site for the stupa near the pond in front of Johnstone House. The Samye Ling Victory Stupa was to be built by volunteer labour to Tai Situpa's design.

In 1998 the first brick was laid by Akong Rinpoche while Bernard Provost, Vin Harris and David Hayward lent their advice and experience with a team of builders, notably Tarchin and

Steve Kent, working hard over the years to keep the early stages of the job progressing. Akong Rinpoche then asked Chenden to take charge of the next more difficult stage which involved finding ways to interpret the traditional Tibetan form of the stupa using western building techniques and materials. He also specified that Chenden should find building methods that would employ the maximum number of people so that they would be able to gain merit from the virtuous activity. In the meantime, well known mountaineers Doug Scott, Sir Chris Bonnington, Hamish MacInnes and Jim Fotheringham joined in the fund raising efforts by leading sponsored treks in the Himalayas.

While work continued on the large stupa a series of eight smaller stupas were built along the entrance driveway, representing the main activities of the Buddha's life. These small stupas were made to traditional designs with the work overseen by Lama Phuntsok, sometimes referred to as the stupa Lama, who together with his team of monks ensured that the stupas were completely authentic. Each one was filled with its own life stick, mantras and precious substances by Akong Rinpoche and Lama Yeshe, together with their guests, Lama Phuntsok from Nepal and Lamdrak Rinpoche from Tibet. They were then consecrated by the Rinpoches and Lamas in a joyful ceremony with members of the sangha playing jahlings, drums and cymbals alternating with chanting as the stupas were blessed one by one. The sight of the gleaming white stupas lining the drive with the copper roofed butter lamp house just behind and the adjacent trees bedecked with many coloured prayer flags made a most auspicious and welcoming entrance to Samye Ling.

During this time work had also been continuing on Phase II and by the summer of 1999 the outer structure had been built. Although there was still a long way to go before the interior would be finished at least the building was up, even though it did rather resemble an airport hangar inside. Nonetheless the Samye Ling community hung the bare breeze block walls with beautiful thangkas and brocades in preparation for a very special event. In Tibet, when a person reaches the age of sixty it is considered to be a very important milestone and as 1999 would mark Akong Rinpoche's sixtieth birthday Lama Yeshe Losal, Sherab Palden and the community wished to pull out all the stops to make it a memorable occasion.

Akong Rinpoche's students gathered from all around the world. Many people had prepared speeches, songs, poems, music and dances to honour Rinpoche on this special day. The cooks at Samye Ling had been busy for days preparing food, including a giant birthday cake. The empty shell of Phase II had been transformed with sumptuous wall hangings, tables laden with food and decorated with flowers and crowds of people filling the place to bursting point. The new wing of Phase II was joyfully inaugurated by this most happy occasion as Akong Rinpoche and his family shared a wonderful birthday feast with the worldwide Samye Ling community. The speeches and entertainment which followed expressed a great outpouring of love and gratitude to Akong Rinpoche for everything he had done to help, not only everyone present but also countless others in the world.

Potala Guest House under construction

Akong Rinpoche on site

Lama Yeshe Losal surveys construction of Phase 2

Samye Ling Shop and Tibetan Tea Rooms

The Butterlamp House and small stupas

Akong Rinpoche and Lamdrak Rinpoche filling the small stupas

The Victory stupa under construction

Building the prayer wheel house

CHAPTER XIII

A NEW MILLENIUM

Samye Ling ushered in the new millennium with the inauguration of the newly completed butter lamp house. After a special, midnight Chenrezig Puja on New Year's Eve, Lama Yeshe Losal made his way from the temple to the butter lamp house where he lit the first lamp and said prayers dedicated to World Peace. He was followed by a long procession of Samye Ling community residents and guests who also lit lamps and made dedications until every one of the 1008 lamps was burning, causing the butter lamp house to blaze with light long into the night. Since then it has been used on a daily basis by people making offerings or dedications for private reasons or for world peace and the happiness of all beings.

Hardly had the new millennium begun when news came through that His Holiness the 17th Karmapa had escaped from Tibet and, after a gruelling journey, had safely arrived in India where he had immediately sought refuge with His Holiness the Dalai Lama at his home in Dharamsala. He was welcomed with open arms by His Holiness who put Gyuto Monastery at the Karmapa's disposal as a base until he could take up his own seat at Rumtek Monastery in Sikkim. The shock waves of His Holiness the Karmapa's daring escape reverberated round the world and the international press soon descended on the tiny Indian village in the Himal Pradesh which had become home for the young head of the Karma Kagyu Lineage.

Although His Holiness was still only fourteen years old and had never been outside Tibet before, his handling of the world media impressed even the most cynical, hard bitten journalists. With a confidence and wisdom that belied his tender years His Holiness explained that he had been obliged to leave Tibet as he had not been given access to his root Lamas, and that if he could not receive teachings from the qualified Lineage Holders then he would be unable to fulfil his spiritual role as the Karmapa. Therefore he had no alternative but to leave Tibet and seek out his principal root Lamas, Their Emminences Tai Situpa and Goshir Gyaltsapa.

Disciples from around the world flocked to Gyuto Monastery to pay their respects to His Holiness and receive his blessing. When people returned to Samye Ling after having met His Holiness they brought blessing cords for the community which seemed to carry waves of blessings and a charge of positive energy. This gave added impetus to the many projects in progress. Work on the large Victory Stupa went into top gear during the summer of 2000 when many volunteers joined the regular crew as the main body of the structure was erected. With the exception of the intricate copper spire made by a specialist firm in Oxford and the ornate, gilded, half ton canopy from Nepal every other part of the stupa had been made at Samye Ling.

In July, Lama Phuntsok, a lineage holder and expert in stupa construction and ritual, arrived from Nepal with five of his monks. After inspecting the structure Lama Phuntsok pronounced it to be one of the most finely executed stupas he'd ever seen. While the final building work continued Lama Phuntsok and his monks performed prayers and blessed the many sacred objects which would fill the upper section of the stupa and give it power. The two essential aspects of the stupa are its architectural shape and the contents, which are housed in the bumpa or vase shaped upper chamber. This had to be filled many priceless treasures including relics of the Buddha and seven full sets of the Kangyur and Tengyur, (the Buddhas' scriptures and commentaries). Other sacred contents include many precious and semi precious stones and metals including coral, turquoise, jade, crystal, lapis lazuli, pearl, gold and silver as well as conch shells, scented woods in treasure vases, copper mandalas, offering bowls, brocades, banners, gilded ornaments, butter lamps and precious relics. Thousands of clay mini stupas, known as Tsa Tsas also had to be made, filled with mantras then hand painted. One hundred and fifty sheets of mantras had to be washed with saffron then dried, rolled and covered in silk. All these sacred objects were brought into the temple to receive the purification and blessing of Lama Phuntsok's ongoing ritual prayers, including the huge life stick, which was intricately carved by Andrew Gordon from a mighty red cedar tree, kindly donated by Jim Lowther of Cumbria.

By August all the contents had been blessed and were ready for the next stage of the ceremony. This was to be in the form of a ten day long Drubchen which would involve continuous prayers for twenty four hours a day throughout the whole period. The great Kagyu Master Sangye Tenzin Rinpoche had been invited to preside over the ceremonies, along with several of his most learned monks. They were joined by a total of fifty other monks, including many Rinpoches and High Lamas who, together with the Samye Ling residents and visitors, participated in this rare and wonderful event. Prayers were chanted to the accompaniment of traditional Tibetan music as the elaborate rites were performed to prescribed, ancient custom. As the various stages of the ceremony unfolded the sacred objects were taken from the temple and carefully placed inside the stupa. The great life stick took twenty people to carry it from the temple on its journey to the stupa where a huge crane carefully lowered it down through the domed roof so it would form the backbone of the structure. The monumental bumpa with all its precious contents safely inside, was then sealed thus becoming a veritable treasure house radiating wholesome and positive energy for the benefit of present and future generations.

Sangye Tenzin Rinpoche then led the entire congregation in a joyous and dignified procession, as cymbals, drums, jahlings and conch shells played, while the long line of people made their way from the temple, around the grounds and pond to finally congregate in front of the impressive stupa with its copper spire topped by a shining silver moon and golden sun. The rituals were performed with Sangye Tenzin Rinpoche concentrating the focus of the High Lamas and all those present as he consecrated the sixty four foot Victory Stupa which would become such a potent and positive force for world peace in the new millennium. Although there was still much work to be done before the stupa would be fully completed it was nevertheless empowered and had all the essential elements and blessings to activate it as a vehicle for overcoming negativity and for radiating positive energy around the universe.

Later that year, Lama Yeshe Losal led a group of ninety people from Samye Ling and various international Samye Dzong branches on a pilgrimage to India. The main part of the pilgrimage was spent at Tai Situpa's monastery of Sherab Ling where the pilgrims received many teachings from Tai Situpa himself and also from Mingyur Rinpoche. The highlights of the trip however were the several visits to see His Holiness the 17th Karmapa who had left Tibet only the year before. Having been given the use of Gyuto Monastery by His Holiness the Dalai Lama, the Karmapa was able to give audiences and teachings to crowds of devotees who flocked to see him from around the world. Given Lama Yeshe's close connection with His Holiness' previous incarnation it was a wonderful opportunity to renew the link with the young Karmapa who made Lama Yeshe and his group extremely welcome. Everyone was overjoyed to meet His Holiness who was so impressive in every way. After giving several enlightened teachings His Holiness also conducted Amitayus empowerment as well as bestowing blessings and keepsakes on each member of the pilgrimage.

During a private audience Lama Yeshe told His Holiness about the Holy Island Project and asked him to give it his blessing. Lama Yeshe explained that the completion of the farmhouse on Holy Island was a major achievement which represented the heart of the planned Centre for World Peace and Health but there was still a substantially greater part of the Project to build from scratch. Raising funds to build two accommodation wings capable of sleeping sixty people and a Peace Hall able to seat up to one hundred was the next challenge. Although Holy Island's many friends and supporters continued to give generous donations it was clear that a much larger sum would have to be raised in order to complete this next ambitious phase of the Project. His Holiness was most interested to hear about Holy Island and even said he would like to visit there one day. He also promised to pray for the Project's fruition.

Holy Island continued to capture the public's imagination and many people made donations towards the Project. Some of these were substantial and occasionally anonymous but Lama Yeshe was unequivocal in attributing all success to the blessing of His Holiness Karmapa. The successful fundraising meant that work could begin in earnest on the Holy Island Centre for World Peace and Health. Because of the scale of the Project and the added difficulties presented by building on a small island, where all supplies and building materials had to be brought over by boat, it was decided that the bulk of this next phase of the Project would be carried out by a professional building firm.

Engineer David Cameron worked on the plans and technical drawings then spent many months applying for planning permission before putting the building work out to tender. After careful consideration Lama Yeshe appointed the Barrs Construction Company to do the job and in the spring of 2002 the heavy duty diggers and earth moving machinery disembarked onto Holy Island and lumbered their way up the beach like great industrial dinosaurs on their way to some Titanic clash. In the following months the ground was prepared and the foundations dug. For quite some time the site behind the farmhouse resembled a vast archaeological dig as pipes were laid and other essential groundwork carried out. Then quite suddenly the building began to rise up.

The long since renovated farmhouse, which was to the fore of the site, began to sprout a huge pair of skeletal wings. Soon the infrastructure of girders and beams were fleshed out by bricks and slates as the building took shape. The Holy Island Project had always been committed to ecologically aware development and the new buildings used shredded recycled paper for insulation, solar panels for heating and a reed bed system for dealing with waste. Even the masonry paint was non toxic. Indeed every effort was made to make as little impact as possible on the environment and for the resulting building to function in harmony with nature.

In the spring of 2002 the exterior construction of the dining and accommodation wings was completed. The focus then switched to building the Peace Hall which, being parallel to the farmhouse would make up the fourth side of the quadrangle enclosing a central courtyard garden. The Peace Hall was designed as the main communal area of the whole project and would be a multi functional space capable of seating over a hundred people. It could be used for a variety of courses, conferences, interfaith gatherings and any other activity that required an airy, spacious venue. As work progressed on the Centre for World Peace and Health at the north end of Holy Island preparations for an equally historic, albeit quieter endeavour began at the south end.

The first light house cottage had been renovated some time ago and consisted of living quarters for care takers and gardeners, as well as several rooms allocated for visitors doing short retreats. More recently the second of the lighthouse cottages had been beautifully refurbished to provide eight bedrooms, bathrooms and a new kitchen and dining area. The out houses had also been renovated to give an additional four bedrooms and what had been the old Victorian boiler room had been gutted and refurbished as a beautiful, new shrine room. Everything was in place for the first Holy Island long term retreat to begin.

Having been given all the necessary empowerments by Kenchen Thrangu Rinpoche at Samye Ling during the summer, an international group of twelve women, from England, Scotland, France, Germany, America and South Africa, converged on Holy Island in the autumn of 2002. After a hair cutting ceremony and pep talks from Retreat Master Lama Yeshe Losal the women walked the boundary which marked the circumference of the vajra tent, or retreat area, which was to be their home for the next three and a half years then stepped inside the door which was duly locked by their Retreat Master. As with the previous retreats at Purelands the participants would follow a strict regime according to the traditional Tibetan Buddhist retreat system, to learn and apply the precious practices of the Kagyu Lineage for the benefit of all sentient beings.

Several of the participants had done previous long retreats, including Chokyi, a long term practitioner who had already completed two such retreats. Her experience would enable her to help the new people on a day to day basis, while Lama Zangmo, who had already completed three previous retreats, would pay frequent visits to give teachings on the various practices. Since completing eleven years of retreat Lama Zangmo had been appointed to set up and run the Samye Dzong Centre in London and had been so successful in establishing this important Centre and helping the many people who use it that she was honoured with the title of Lama. Akong Rinpoche does not bestow the title of Lama lightly and Lama Zangmo is only one of three such people to have received it from him, the others being Lama Jinpa and Lama Tsondreu from Spain.

The Holy Island retreatants were also fortunate to receive visits from Mingyur Rinpoche, Khenpo Tsultrim Gyamsto Rinpoche, Akong Rinpoche and Lama Yeshe Losal Rinpoche, all of whom gave many precious teachings. The island itself provided the perfect, sacred environment for retreat, and even though the retreatants were not allowed to roam at will, the unobstructed views of sea, sky and mountain provided a sense of peace and spaciousness to inspire their practice.

Although the retreatants were in strict seclusion from the outside world, they did occasionally receive requests for prayers. Their prayers dedicated to world peace could scarcely have been more needed as the world reeled from the aftermath of events following 9/11, with war breaking out in Afghanistan and Iraq. Lama Yeshe Losal, always such a positive force for good, spread his message of inner peace leading to world peace as he travelled the globe. Whether conducting a modest interfaith gathering inside a yurt on Holy Island or attending top level meetings with royalty and dignitaries from all major faiths in Buckingham Palace, Lambeth Palace, and the Commonwealth Office Lama Yeshe Losal was becoming a familiar and much respected figure in interfaith circles. His ambition to build the Holy Island Centre for World Peace and Health as a sacred space of peace and harmony open to people of all faiths was fast becoming a reality and on May 31st 2003 the new Centre opened its doors to the public for the very first time.

The ferry boat men ran a continual shuttle service to the island bringing wave after wave of visitors, ranging from VIP's and Press to hundreds of curious locals from the nearby Isle of Arran who were eager to see what exactly had been going on for the last year on their neighbouring island. As guests disembarked and made their way up the beach past a row of gleaming white stupas leading towards the Centre they were met by a beaming Lama Yeshe who took great pleasure in conducting a guided tour of the new buildings and grounds. The Lama's evident delight with the Centre was matched by the visitors' reactions to it as they admired the beautifully decorated rooms, the spacious dining room with its oak refectory tables and log fire stove, the light and airy Peace Hall with its wood panelled walls and sky lit roof and the landscaped gardens which were in full bloom.

Since then the Holy Island Centre for World Peace and Health has gone from strength to strength hosting annual interfaith gatherings, running a wide range of popular courses throughout the spring, summer and autumn and remaining open during the winter as a place of retreat and meditation. It is run in a professional but caring way by a group of volunteer residents whose numbers are augmented in the summer months by a wonderful group of volunteers who keep the place running like clockwork so that visitors enjoy every comfort, wonderful food, a friendly atmosphere and of course the beauty of a totally natural island environment to explore.

With the Centre at the north end of the island fulfilling its function as a place of peace, health and interfaith harmony and the long term Women's Retreat progressing well at the south end the focus of the island's building team shifted to Glenscorrodale on the Isle of Arran. Situated in a peaceful valley threaded by a silvery stream the picturesque Glenscorrodale farmhouse was in a parlous condition and its outhouses damp and barely standing. David Cameron had drawn up plans according to Lama Yeshe's instructions and had obtained planning permission for the work to proceed. Most of the building team were monks and lay volunteers who had to stay in caravans while they worked at demolishing the derelict old house and rotten sheds in preparation for the building of the long term Men's Retreat. Many of the team, who had previously worked on Holy Island, had a vested interest in the project as they had already signed up for the long retreat but couldn't begin until the building was complete.

It was a slow process as there was so much to do and the living conditions were very tough in the early days. Winters could be pretty grim living in leaky caravans then working all day in rain and howling winds. Work could proceed apace in the summer months but even that brought its difficulties, as anyone who has encountered the Scottish midge will attest. Nonetheless, the intrepid crew would don their green net midgie masks and set to work looking like a band of convicts in the Australian outback. Deadlines came and went as the work went on, often beset by bad weather and other difficulties. Finally in the spring of 2004, after a no nonsense phone call from Akong Rinpoche in Spain, it became clear that the already exhausted crew would have to extend themselves even more and work seven days a week to meet the final deadline.

Fortunately Lama Yeshe arrived to lend a hand and keep spirits up as the team battled against the clock to get the building finished. Matters were not helped when an untimely flood caused the nearby stream to break its banks, damaging a bridge and causing floodwater to engulf the building site and break apart a system of pipes. It was as if nature itself was testing the men's resolve. Thoughts of Milarepa and his seemingly endless task of building structures for his teacher Marpa sprang to mind. Much to their credit the men's will and dedication drove them on and in the last few weeks before the deadline everything suddenly came together to result in a beautiful, brand new, purpose built retreat centre.

Akong Rinpoche arrived with a crowd of well wishers who came to see the gleaming new shrine room and retreat buildings and to say their farewells to the twenty men about to enter retreat for the next four years. Once the friends and families had left Akong Rinpoche cut the retreatants hair then gave them a rather vigorous blessing with a sacred stone and a sprinkle of holy water to get their retreat off to an auspicious start. There were still a few last jobs needing to be done in order to complete the painting and decorating but they were somehow worked in to the daily retreat schedule and accomplished in true Karma Kagyu fashion as part of the practice of purification and accumulation.

While all this activity had been happening on Holy Island and at Glenscorrodale, Samye Ling's own building programme had also been making great progress. A second row of eight small stupas had been built opposite the existing eight on the other side of the entrance drive. Together they formed an avenue of stupas that welcome visitors as they arrive. On the 26th of May 2002 Akong Rinpoche conducted the ceremony to fill the stupas with the sacred mantras and precious contents before sealing and consecrating them. As the event took place on a full moon day commemorating the Buddha's enlightenment and parinirva Rinpoche said it was particularly auspicious and that merit from such virtuous activities would be multiplied by 100,000. Later that day Akong Rinpoche gave the initiation and authorisation for the practice of Chenrezig to hundreds of people who filled the temple to receive his blessing.

With the exterior construction of the south wing of Phase II having also been completed it became possible for most of the interior work to be done by volunteers. Akong Rinpoche would often be found on the building site, grey with plaster dust as he worked with indomitable will along side men half his age, creating a hive of activity. The first part of Phase II to be totally completed was the self contained apartment which would be used for visiting High Lamas and other dignitaries. The Samye Ling building and decorating crew worked almost round the clock to finish the decoration and furnishing with only minutes to spare before the arrival of a Tibetan Princess and her family who were to be the first honoured guests.

Lama Yeshe Losal and Ringu Tulku lighting butterlamps

His Holiness the 17th Karmpa

The Victory Stupa

Sir Chris Bonnington and Lama Phuntsok

Larma Yeshe on site at the newly constructed Holy Island Centre

The Peace Hall

The Holy Island Centre for World Peace and Health

The Women's Retreat

Men's retreat shrine room

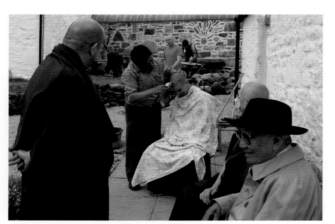

Prepartions for the men's retreat

Lama Yeshe Losal with Interfaith Representatives

Akong Rinpoche with Mother Theresa

H.R.H. Prince of Wales

H.R.H. Princess Anne

His Holiness the Pope with Lama Yeshe Losal

Lama Yeshe with H.R.H Duke of Edinburgh and Interfaith representatives

The Archbishop of Canterbury

CHAPTER XIV

FRUITION

Princess Rigzin Zangmo, daughter of the late Panchen Lama, came to visit Samye Ling with her mother in August 2002 as part of an international tour which would culminate in Tibet. The Princess, who was educated in the U.S., is a much revered figure in her homeland and spoke very eloquently at the Rokpa annual general meeting, describing her plans to help the people of Tibet. She also attended the Samye Ling open day and tea party along with Lord David Steel and the Church of Scotland Moderator as well as a large crowd of visitors who turned out to enjoy the afternoon tea, entertainments and summer sunshine while admiring the latest additions to the Samye Ling buildings and gardens.

Some of the most notable changes were those to the stupa and its surroundings. Thanks to the considerable craftsmanship of Karpu and Pema Dorje, who had been specially invited over from Nepal, the exterior of the stupa and the adjacent Guru Rinpoche fountain of blessings had been embellished with extremely beautiful carvings. At the same time, Jinpa, a master cabinet maker who had previously been a monk on Holy Island, had made the entire shrine for the interior of the stupa. Using native woods such as cherry, yew and oak Jinpa created a most exquisite inner sanctum with wood panelled cabinets lining the walls, which would hold sandalwood boxes to contain the ashes of people who had died. The shrine itself was adorned by four pillars of polished sycamore inlaid with ebony and the whole room was finished to a degree of fine craftsmanship that is rarely encountered in modern times.

As one of the main uses of the stupa shrine would be to help people through the immediate post death experience it had been designed as an Amitabha shrine, since he is the Buddha of Dewachen heaven and is closest to our human realm. The central Amitabha statue would be flanked by the figures of Vajrapani and Chenrezig and fill the whole west side of the shrine. In order to make these of the highest standard Akong Rinpoche had invited master artist and sculptor Lama Thubten Kunsal to come over from Tibet. It was incredible to see the speed and skill of the artist at work. The clay seemed to come alive in his hands as the graceful forms of the Buddha and Boddhisattvas emerged as if by magic. Working steadily throughout the winter months the master artist completed all three of these major statues which now adorn the stupa shrine.

Lama Thubten Kunsal then turned his attention to the fountain of blessings which was waiting to receive its main figure of Guru Rinpoche. Having erected a scaffold over the circular pool, Thubten Kunsal assisted by Gyamtso, Karpu and Pema Dorje, set about creating the large figure of Padmasambava, or Guru Rinpoche, sitting on a lotus rising out of the pool. Once again, Thubten Kunsal's artistry resulted in a majestically impressive figure, adorned with all the marks and accoutrements of Guru Rinpoche. In the following spring the statue was beautifully painted in great detail and the fountain filled with water entering through the mouth of a carved dragon, into the pool and overflowing out via a naga, through a vase and down a miniature waterfall to trickle into the pond below, creating a most delightful water sculpture.

The stupa itself has already been used as a place of prayer for Samye Ling residents who have died, notably Rinpoche's former secretary Dee Croft, Gwen Millward, Monica Gerling, Tara Rokpa therapist Lorna Watson, artist Monica Tinley, Michael Tuck and the Portuguese monk Karma Tenpa. In recent years all of these much loved members of the community were laid in their coffins inside the stupa while monks, nuns and lay people took it in turns to say prayers and keep vigil day and night for three days leading up to the funerals. The peaceful, sacred space of the stupa, so full of blessings, provides the perfect place to say goodbye to loved ones and to pray for their auspicious rebirth. It is thanks to Akong Rinpoche's and Lama Yeshe's vision and to the hard work of everyone involved in the Stupa Project that Samye Ling now has this most beautiful place in which to mark the end of one life and help transition into the next.

In December 2002 Samye Ling was honoured to receive a visit from Yongey Mingyur Dorje Rinpoche. This eminent teacher is the eighth incarnation of his line and although still in his twenties has already completed many years of study and several long term retreats, having been appointed as Retreat Master by Tai Situpa at Sherab Ling Monastery where he is based. Mingyur Dorje bestowed empowerments for the practice of Amitabha and Dorje Phurba. He then led a five day long Dorje Phurba Drubcho Ceremony, on the advice of Tai Situpa, in order to dispel obstacles and negative influences. The Drubcho included prayers for the dead and Ruchok, which is the preparation of their ashes into tsa tsa for ceremonial placing inside the Samye Ling stupa.

Another landmark event was the celebration of the 60th birthday of Lama Yeshe Losal and the 90th birthday of Sherab Palden Beru. It had been Akong Rinpoche's wish that these important birthdays should be celebrated in what would become the new dining room in Phase II. In order to achieve this goal the volunteer builders focused all their efforts on finishing the interior of the huge space, which would be capable of seating three hundred people. Once again everyone worked for many months with tremendous dedication to finish this most ambitious building to a very high standard.

On the afternoon of August 9th 2003 the concrete shell had been transformed into a beautifully decorated, light and airy dining hall adorned with decorative ceiling panels, thangkas and Tibetan carpets, ready to receive Lama Yeshe Losal, Sherab Palden and of course Akong Rinpoche who made the first speech in honour of their birthdays, addressing the hundreds of people who had gathered for the happy occasion. Rinpoche was evidently pleased with his younger brother's achievements at Samye Ling and made a point of saying that Lama Yeshe could be addressed as Rinpoche if people felt inclined to do so. He explained that the title Rinpoche meant precious one and could be used of great and accomplished teachers, not only tulkus.

There followed much joyous entertainment with speeches, songs, dances and presentations to Lama Yeshe Losal Rinpoche, including that of a long life prayer written especially for him by His Holiness the 17th Karmapa. Lama Yeshe Rinpoche then cut an enormous birthday cake which was distributed to the hundreds of well wishers, and made his own speech to thank everyone. He particularly expressed his gratitude to the people who had worked so hard to get the new dining room ready and added his wish that all Samye Ling's friends and supporters would continue to put their energy into completing the rest of Phase II so that Akong Rinpoche's vision for a fully equipped Monastery and Tibetan Centre would be realised for the benefit of all beings.

After the tea party and entertainments guests wandered in the summer sunshine, enjoying the Peace Garden with its stupa, sculptures, pools and fountain set amongst the lawns, shady trees and flowers in full bloom. The latest addition to the Samye Ling gardens was a second pond situated to the south of the existing one. In its centre the resplendent golden figure of Nagarjuna, shielded by a great hooded cobra, sits in meditation, his mirror image reflected in the rippling water of the beautiful lotus studded pond. Being the source of the Mahayana Buddhism that Padmasambhava introduced to Tibet, Nagarjuna is a particularly important figure in Tibetan Buddhism. Akong Rinpoche had asked Lama Thubten Kunsal to build the statue facing west and thereby symbolise the seeds of Mahayana Buddhism taking root in the western world. As the sun set on this most happy and auspicious day everyone gravitated to the Nagarjuna lotus pond which provided the perfect backdrop for a spectacular firework display kindly sponsored by the members of London Samye Dzong community, to honour Lama Yeshe Rinpoche's birthday.

Later that month Mingyur Rinpoche returned to Samye Ling and after a weekend of public talks and a Vajrasattva empowerment gave the first Mahamudra teachings to a large group of students who had taken the commitment to complete a three year course. Mingyur Rinpoche generously offered to visit Samye Ling on a yearly basis in order to give the essential instructions on the supreme teachings of Mahamudra. He concluded his visit with another weekend of public talks and ceremonies, including the bestowal of a Marpa Practice Empowerment.

Since the start of the new millennium Mingyur Rinpoche, Khenpo Tsultrim Gyamtso, and Ringu Tulku had all regularly graced Samye Ling with their presence and given many precious teachings. Lama Yeshe Losal also gave invaluable courses in meditation on a biannual basis, but Akong Rinpoche, who always invited the best teachers, could rarely be persuaded to give teachings himself. With much insistence on the part of those putting together the Samye Ling course programme he occasionally consented to give an empowerment, but so rare were his teachings that many of the newer Samye Ling residents had never actually heard him speak. It was with great joy and astonishment therefore that people received the news of his sudden decision to lead a two week teaching retreat. News spread like wildfire and the course was attended to capacity by students from all around the world.

The teachings were held in July 2004 in the meeting hall section of the new dining room block. People sat facing Akong Rinpoche, who was informally seated in an armchair, smiling with a twinkle in his eye as if to say, "You asked for it, now you've got it." Rinpoche then taught some of the most profound meditation exercises of the Nyingma tradition then proceeded to give teachings based on a root text of Patrul Rinpoche's dealing with the five mind poisons. In his direct and inimitable style Rinpoche illuminated the text with the minimum of words and the maximum of meaning. Knowing how easy it is for people to listen without really absorbing, Akong Rinpoche then asked everyone to learn the essence of the text by heart. In the following days he would pick people at random to stand up and recite what they had memorised. Interspersed with the teachings Akong Rinpoche gave empowerments during the weekends of this precious time. For Rinpoche's long term students, as well as those who had never before attended his teachings the retreat was a time of revelation and great blessing. As with his five week teaching retreat given in the early seventies and the three week retreat of '85 it was a memorable turning point in many peoples' lives.

Less than a year later the Samye Ling international community once again converged on the 'Mother Centre' this time to participate in an Easter Course of 2005 which included Guru Rinpoche and Vajrasattva empowerments, a three day long Guru Rinpoche Drubcho and a celebration of Akong Rinpoche's 65th Birthday. As well as the usual birthday feast and entertainments, courtesy of hundreds of well wishers, the day was also celebrated with the release of three thousand brown trout into the river Esk as people made their good wishes for Akong Rinpoche's long life.

Fortunately Akong Rinpoche continues to enjoy good health and boundless energy. This was very much in evidence that summer when he headed a group of volunteers to work on yet another building project. A prayer wheel house had been designed to surround the stupa in a U shaped building so that people could turn the prayer wheels as they made their koras of the stupa, thus sending the positive energy of millions of mantras contained inside the wheels to all parts of the universe. New volunteers worked alongside old hands such as Vin Harris and Bernard Provost, Dave Hayward and Gary Buckley. George Briggs, a veteran of many previous Samye Ling building projects, co-ordinated the work and as usual, Akong Rinpoche's presence on the building site served to inspire everyone with his indefatigable example. By autumn the building was almost complete then work was brought to a halt for the winter with the intention to add the finishing touches in the following spring.

However, during a winter cold spell, an empty logging lorry travelling along the road bordering Samye Ling hit a treacherous patch of black ice and careered off the road, through the hedge and crashed into the newly built prayer wheel house, coming to rest just inches away from the stupa. Lama Yeshe Rinpoche and others had been doing their early morning kora only minutes before and it is something of a miracle that neither they, nor indeed the lorry driver were injured. The stupa too remained unscathed, thanks to the prayer wheel house which had acted as a protection barrier and was badly damaged. The lorry was a write off. Once the lorry had been extricated and the site cleared up it was left until the spring before rebuilding could commence.

The spring of 2006 was a memorable time, particularly on Holy Island as it marked the completion of the first long term Women's Retreat in the island's history. An unseasonably heavy snowfall in March was regarded as an auspicious sign by the retreatants as they performed the concluding ceremonies. Unlike the completions of the previous retreats at Purelands, where the retreatants walked in procession to be greeted by families and well wishers at Samye Ling, the inaccessability and seclusion of the island made such ceremony impossible. However, the retreatants hoped that Akong Rinpoche , Lama Yeshe Rinpoche and Lama Zangmo would be there to officially open the retreat boundary. The severe weather made travel to the island almost impossible and caused the Rinpoches and Lama Zangmo to have to dig their vehicle out of a snow drift en route to the ferry. The extreme conditions meant they had to spend two unscheduled nights in hotels and it began to look as if Akong Rinpoche would not be able to get to Holy Island as he was due to fly to Spain the following day. The retreatants were understanding but very disappointed and prayed for a break in the weather so that the Rinpoches could cross safely to the island. The usual ferry service was unable to sail in the rough seas but by some miracle the skipper of the lifeboat dinghy returned that day from holiday and not only brought the party over, but also took Rinpoche back the same day so that he could catch his plane to Spain. The few hours Rinpoche was able to spend on the island with the retreatants were precious indeed and everyone was immensely grateful to him and Lama Yeshe Rinpoche for the huge effort they had made in order to be present at the conclusion of the three and a half year retreat.

When the retreatants returned to Samye Ling they were amazed to see all the many changes to the buildings and gardens that had occurred during their absence. As well as all the previously mentioned changes an impressive ceremonial gateway had also been built as an alternative entrance to the complex. The vegetable growing gardens had been extended and a new structure erected for the purpose of drying and processing the many medicinal and culinary herbs cultivated in the garden. The Prayer Wheel House had been rebuilt and would soon be completed. Lama Thubten Kunsal had created a beautiful statue of a 1000 arm Chenrezig and was busy putting the finishing touches to statues of Guru Rinpoche and of His Holiness Rigpe Dorje the 16th Karmapa. These three will be the focal point of a thousand armed Chenrezig shrine in what had been the original shrine room in Johnstone House before the temple was built. Having since been used as an office for the Rinpoches the room will soon revert to being a shrine dedicated for the practice of Nyungneys.

The temple itself had also undergone further enhancement with the addition of an intricately carved niche behind the main Buddha statue with miniature Buddha figures on lotus thrones depicting all the main events of Lord Buddha's lifetime. New, richly woven, Tibetan carpets for seating also added to the feeling of comfort for the many visitors coming to participate in prayer and meditation. One of the most exquisite additions to the temple was to be found on the top most level where a beautiful Medicine Buddha shrine had been created in the relic room. Lapis blue carpets lead to the richly carved shrine where the golden figure of the Medicine Buddha sits serene and impassive, surrounded by numerous smaller Medicine Buddha statues showing different symbolic mudras

The upper floor of Phase II had also been completed to provide a spacious new Abbot's office and audience room as well as comfortable accommodation for resident long term monks and visiting Lamas. The completion of the Lamas apartment and the new monks' quarters was most timely for in May 2006 two Lamas from Palpung Monastery in Tibet and one from Sherab Ling Monastery in India came to Samye Ling at the invitation of Akong Rinpoche and Lama Yeshe Rinpoche in order to instruct the western sangha and lay community. His Holiness the 17th Karmapa had requested that all Kagyu monasteries should standardise their pujas so that they were all conducting them in the same way. Lama Norbu, a superb umze, gave instructions on the chanting and cymbals, Dance Master Lama Karil taught jahlings and sacred dance while the expert Shrine Master Lama Tsenor taught shrine duties and how to make all the offerings needed for daily and monthly pujas.

Several weeks later some fifteen more monks arrived from Sherab Ling in order to start preparations for the forthcoming Guru Rinpoche Drubcho at Samye Ling, and for the Vajrakilaya Drubchen which would follow on Holy Island. It was wonderful to welcome so many dharma brothers to Samye Ling and to be able to learn so much from them. A hectic but joyous time ensued with so many classes going on all day, in amongst the making of hundreds of intricate tormas, elaborate dance masks, costumes and countless other preparations for the important ceremonies ahead.

As the day of the Drubcho drew nearer activities were reaching fever pitch in an effort to get everything ready. Then, just a few days before the ceremony was to begin the great Lama who was to preside over the Drubcho, the 18th Dulmo Choje Rinpoche arrived from Tibet accompanied by Pasang Tulku Trinley. The tall, impressive figure of Dulmo Choje Rinpoche emanated a serene calm and a quietly contagious confidence that everything that needed to be accomplished would be.

The Drubcho duly began on June 20th with the Samye Ling shrine room packed to the rafters with Rinpoches and monks from Tibet and India, the western sangha, the resident community and hundreds of guests who had all gathered to participate in this most auspicious ten day ceremony. The purpose of the Guru Rinpoche Drubcho was to alleviate all forms of suffering. Using the power of prayer, sacred music, dance and ancient ritual the Drubcho would act as a spiritual magnet attracting positive and peaceful energy to balance the elements and overcome sickness, famine, war and other negative influences.

The wisdom and skilful means of the High Lamas, allied with the faith and dedication of all the participants created a pure and wholesome offering, a joyous celebration and a noble aspiration for world peace. It was also a rare opportunity to witness this powerful tradition and was a life changing event for many of the people who attended. The ceremony culminated in a series of ritual dances which took place in a traditional Tibetan open sided tent specially erected for the occasion in front of the temple. The months of dance classes, costume and mask making finally came to fruition as the dancers leapt and whirled around in a blaze of colour and exotic masks, breathing life into the archetypal figures.

Barely had the dust settled from Guru Rinpoche Drubcho when preparations started for an even more elaborate event scheduled to take place on Holy Island. This was to be a full scale two week long Vajrakilaya Drubchen which would also be lead by Dulmo Choje Rinpoche. As it would involve a vast number of highly complex offering tormas an advanced party of torma makers, lead by shrine master Lama Tsenor, travelled to Holy Island to start work. Meanwhile, a team of carpenters constructed a huge wooden mandala which would be the focal point for the ceremonies. Everything that was needed for the Drubchen had to be carefully packed and transported by boat then unpacked on the island and assembled.

The spacious Peace Hall was transformed into a Tibetan Buddhist shrine room with the huge scarlet mandala in the centre adorned with banners and embroidered hangings and flanked by a high throne for Dulmo Choje Rinpoche and rows of carpets and cushions on either side for the monks, nuns and lay people. The mandala was then filled with hundreds of phurbas, ritual objects, tormas, offering bowls and lights. The ceremonies went on day and night throughout the whole time, not only in the main shrine room but also in two others that had been constructed in a side room off the Peace Hall and in the small shrine room above the Heritage Centre a little way up the beach. There were also numerous fire pujas and masked dances performed at various intervals throughout the two weeks, making for a veritable multiplex of auspicious activity and wondrous complexity.

With Dulmo Choje Rinpoche and the other Lamas' inspiring examples it was a time of full on commitment, hard work, little sleep and great blessing. The weather was perfect with day after day of clear blue skies, enabling meals to be eaten outside on the terrace with stunning sea and mountain views to delight the eyes. The island's volunteer cooks and staff also contributed greatly to the success of the proceedings and ensured that the whole affair ran smoothly. Lama Yeshe Rinpoche was in his element and was undoubtedly very happy to see his vision of Holy Island become manifest in such a spectacular and joyful occasion. The event will doubtless live on in the memories of all those who were fortunate enough to attend, not least the energetic young monks of Sherab Ling, whose appetite for hard work was matched only by their exuberant play as they would find time for an after puja game of beach football followed by a cooling, late evening swim.

On returning to Samye Ling the Palpung Lamas and Sherab Ling monks had only one day to gather their belongings before leaving for London and boarding their flights back to India and Tibet. Many of them had been at Samye Ling for the best part of the summer and it was a little sad to see these new friends leave. Nonetheless they had given the community so many happy memories and valuable lessons, particularly Lamas Norbu, Karil and Tsenor whose influence on chanting, music and shrine duties lives on in the many pujas regularly performed at Samye Ling.

Akong Rinpoche also departed for Tibet and a few months later Lama Yeshe Rinpoche left for the Men's Retreat on the Isle of Arran where he spent three months on retreat and serving as a great inspiration to the men who were by then in their second year of retreat. Life at Samye Ling went on as usual throughout the autumn, then as winter set in the pace began to quicken in readiness for Lama Yeshe Rinpoche's return. As Christmas approached the number of visitors started to increase in readiness for Lama Yeshe Rinpoche's ever popular Christmas Retreat and meditation course. Despite gale force winds and frequent power cuts the course was a great success, attracting not only Buddhists but people from many other faiths who had come to Samye Ling to escape the commercialisation of Christmas and spend it in a more peaceful and spiritual way. On New Years Eve everyone gathered in the shrine room to attend a late night Chenrezig Puja and as 2006 became 2007 Lama Yeshe Rinpoche led a procession of people out from the temple to the butterlamp house to offer lights dedicated to world peace.

A month later, to the great joy of the Samye Ling community, Akong Rinpoche returned from Tibet. On a clear, crisp winter's night crowds of people gathered at the gate and lined the driveway flanked by stupas and the butterlamp house which was twinkling with the flames of 1008 lamps. As Rinpoche's car pulled up and he emerged wreathed in smiles, looking younger and healthier than ever, everyone queued up to offer him their kattas and welcome him home.

At the time of writing Samye Ling is preparing for Losar and the Tibetan New Year celebrations on Febrary 18th 2007. This will be followed by the empowerment of one thousand armed Chenrezig, bestowed by Akong Rinpoche, in preparation for the annual Nyungney Retreat, in which he will also participate. The Nyungneys are a time of purification, a means to generate compassion and a most auspicious way to start the New Year. In particular, this year of the Fire Pig is a very special time for Samye Ling as it marks the 40th anniversary.

Akong Tulku Rinpoche and Lama Yeshe Rinpoche, together with an entourage of Samye Sangha, will spend the early part of the year travelling to the Samye Dzong branches around the world, in order to celebrate the 40th anniversary with ceremonies in each place. They will then return to Samye Ling in the summer when it is hoped that many of Samye Ling's family members from across the globe will reunite to join in a series of events which will honour Samye Ling's anniversary. This will include the Guru Rinpoche initiation given by Akong Rinpoche on July 6th, then the special ten day long Guru Rinpoche Drubcho starting on July 24th followed by the annual open day and tea party on Sunday August 5th.

A letter of invitation has been sent to His Holiness the 17th Karmapa and we have every hope that this may be the year that His Holiness makes his first visit to the West. His presence at Samye Ling would be the most perfect gift for the celebration of this 40th anniversary. Whether or not His Holiness is able to come this year we pray for his long life and for the elimination of all obstacles so that he may soon visit Europe, and Kagyu Samye Ling in particular, thereby benefiting countless more beings. Karmapa Chenno.

Photo by Murdo MacLeod

Guru Rinpoche Drubcho

Photo by Brian Stewart

Nagarjuna

Photo by Anna Branthwaite

Lama Thubten Kunsal at work

Photo by Colin McPherson

Guru Rinpoche Fountain of Blessings

118

Interior shrine of the stupa

Photo by Brian Stewart

Victory stupa and prayer wheel house

Guru Rinpoche Drubcho 2006

Dakini Dancers

Dulmo Choje Rinpoche

Photos by Anna Branthwaite

Masked dancer

Photo by Sam Scoggins

Vajrakilaya Drubchen on Holy Island

Akong Rinpoche with the Nyungney Retreat Group 2007

CHAPTER XV

INTO THE FUTURE

To conclude the story of Kagyu Samye Ling's forty year history it is only fitting to leave the final words to the two extraordinary brothers without whom Samye Ling would never have become what it is today. It is thanks to their complete devotion to His Holiness Karmapa and their utter compassion for all beings that Samye Ling has caused Buddhadharma to flourish in the West and has benefited so many people. May their lives be long and fruitful that their wisdom and compassion continue to shine like the sun, illuminating the lives of all beings.

Lama Yeshe Losal Rinpoche

"As many people know, Samye Ling was named after Samye, the first Buddhist Monastery and Cultural Centre to be established in Tibet. In the same way, the aim of Samye Ling has been to establish Buddhism in the West and after the last forty years we can look back and see that so many people have already been helped from following the authentic Kagyu Lineage of Mahamudra. Just as the Tibetan Samye has existed for many centuries and still continues to benefit beings I pray that Samye Ling will have a similar, long lasting influence, truly establishing the Kagyu Lineage here on a foundation of unconditional loving kindness, wisdom and compassion for the benefit of all beings.

In order to achieve this goal I hope all the friends and supporters of Samye Ling will pool their energy and resources to complete Samye Project's third and final phase in accordance with my brother Akong Rinpoche's wishes. Phase III will form the educational wing of Samye Ling consisting of extensive Tibetan and English Buddhist libraries, a museum to house many sacred relics and artefacts, an audio visual department to record precious teachings and a Buddhist College affiliated to a prestigious British university for the study of Tibetan Buddhism. It will also provide accommodation for life ordained nuns to match the existing monk's accommodation in Phase II. Of course all this does not come cheaply. We will need to raise in the region of £5 million. We should not be daunted by the expense but just be positive and do whatever we can to realise Rinpoche's vision.

People may think that wealth, possessions and fame would make them happy, but we can already see that all the choice and material goods of this modern age often lead to more unhappiness and problems. Lord Buddha saw that selfishness, ignorance and greed are destructive for ourselves and others, which is why Buddhism is more relevant today than ever. We are now experiencing the result of ignorant behaviour that has damaged our planet and is causing pollution, catastrophic weather and global warming. As a Buddhist Lama I will do whatever I can to ensure that Samye Ling develops in an environmentally conscious way. We are currently re-insulating Johnstone House and fitting solar panels as well as planting many more trees at Samye Ling and on Holy Island and at Glenscorrodale. Lama Thubten Kunsal will soon finish the beautiful statue he is making of Green Tara in the garden then we will plant an orchard of fruit trees around her to create a lovely grove which will be a wonderful addition to our landscaped grounds that not only give pleasure to residents and visitors but also attract more birds and wildlife.

However, the best investment for our future and that of our planet is based on people following the Dharma. That is why I am so keen to provide the right conditions for people to do retreat. It is important that men and women practitioners who wish to dedicate their lives to the Dharma should be given the ways and means to do so and not be prevented by lack of resources. Some people may not have the time or circumstances to do retreat themselves but may be able to sponsor others. According to Buddhism anyone who sponsors a committed practitioner to do retreat gains the equivalent benefit themselves. In this way I hope that many people will help Buddhadharma truly take root and blossom in the West for the happiness of all sentient beings"

Akong Tulku Rinpoche

"My wish is to benefit people in whatever way is possible. That is what I do. In the immediate future of Samye Ling I would like to finish what we have started and complete Phase III which will provide full Buddhist educational facilities as well as better accommodation. Another aspect of education we wish to encourage concerns care for the environment and we will be building an eco cabin where schools and other groups visiting Samye Ling can get information and hands on experience of sustainable energy resources working in harmony with nature. We are also hoping to acquire some nearby land with the idea of turning it into a conservation area for wildlife and wild flowers.

As we are all getting older many of our community members will need more healthcare and comfortable accommodation with easy access. Therefore we have a project to create some sheltered housing, purpose built to cater for the needs of the elderly with a health clinic and spa on site. It is so important to look after our elders as we would wish to be looked after when the time comes. They have so much to give the younger generation and should be treated with care and respect.

I have no idea of my work ever finishing. I always look to see what is needed and if there is a demand for more projects then that is what I do, according to needs. It is an ongoing situation. In this life, when one thing finishes another one begins, so there is constant activity. There is no end."

Akong Rinpoche at work on the plans for Phase III with (left to right), David Hayward, George Briggs, Bernard Provost, Gary Buckley and Vin Harris. With the exception of George Briggs who is project co-ordinator, the group were all key members of the building team that created the Samye Ling temple. Twenty years on they are reuniting and lending their expertise to lead volunteer builders in the construction of Phase III in order to complete the Samye Project.

Artist's impression of the completed Kagyu Samye Ling outlining the yet to be built Phase III. For information and updates on the Samye Project visit www.samyeling.org To make a donation towards this all important final phase of the Samye Project please contact admin@samyeling.org

"To build temples and places where wisdom, truth and compassion may flourish will generate much virtue. Such virtue is incalculable since it will carry on being generated for as long as even one stone or brick of the building continues to exist" Buddhist scripture.

CHAPTER XVI

PRECIOUS TEACHINGS GIVEN AT SAMYE LING

The following chronological list of teachings from 1972 onwards is not exhaustive but is the best that could be established from existing records.

YEAR	TEACHER	TOPIC
1972	Very Ven. Khenpo Kalu Rinpoché	general dharma teachings/ foundationpractices
	Ven. Sochu Suzuki	Zen meditation course
	Ven. Phra Maha Imm	meditation course
1973	Ven. Phra Maha Imm	meditation course
	Ven. Akong Rinpoché	general dharma teachings
1974	Very Ven. Khenpo Kalu Rinpoché	teachings and empowerments
	His Holiness Gyalwa Karmapa	teachings and empowerments
	Sister Khechog Palmo	teachings
	Bikkhu from Thai Vihara	meditation course
1975	Very Ven. Khenpo Kalu Rinpoché	teachings and empowerments
	Geshe Tsultrim Gyaltsen	Tibetan language
	Ven. Dr. Rewatta Dhamma	vipassana course
	Ven. Akong Rinpoché/Lama Urgyen	foundation practices
	Chao Khun Phra Pariyattivarakun	meditation course
1976	Ven. Akong Rinpoché	meditation retreat
1977	Very Ven. Khamtrul Rinpoché	teachings and empowerments
	Ven. Akong Rinpoché	meditation course
	Ven. Lama Lhacho	Chenresig instruction
	H.H. Gyalwa Karmapa	teachings and empowerments
	Jamgon Kongtrul Rinpoché	teachings
1978	Ven. Akong Rinpoché	meditation instruction
	Ven. Lama Lhacho	Chenresig instruction
1979	Dharmacarya Tenpa Negi	Tibetan language
	Ven. Lama Gendun	teachings/empowerments
	Ven. Lama Lhacho	Amitabha practice
	Khenpo Tsultrim Gyamtso	Buddhist philosophy
	Ven. Akong Rinpoché	meditation course
	Sherab Palden Beru	Tibetan art
	Ven. Akong Rinpoché	shamatha retreat
	Dokyu Nagakawa Roshi	Zen course
	Ven. Dr. Saddhutissa	teachings and meditation
	Ven. Dr. Rewatta Dhamma	teachings and meditation
	Ven. Akong Rinpoché	mahayana theory
	Ven. Chime Tulku	mahayana theory
	Khenchen Thrangu Rinpoché	teachings
	Ven. Lama Lhacho	conclusion of 100 million Mani mantras
	Khenpo Tsultrim Gyamtso	Lamcho Rinchen Trengwa'
1980	Khenchen Thrangu Rinpoché	Milarepa course

	Ven. Akong Rinpoché	teachings
	Khenpo Tsultrim Gyamtso	valid cognition
	Dharmacarya Tenpa Negi	Tibetan language
	Ven. Tulku Tenga	Tibetan spiritual arts
	Khenchen Thrangu Rinpoché	**3-MONTH SUMMER SCHOOL**
		'Ornament of Liberation'
		'Mahayana Uttara Tantra'
		Foundation practices
	Ven. Akong Rinpoché	dharma in daily life
1981	the Kunzik Shamarpa	'4-session Guru Yoga'
		'7 Points of Mind Training'
		Madhyamaka theory
		3-MONTH SUMMER SCHOOL
	the Khentin Tai Situpa	Buddhist history
		Kagyu Indian hagiographies
		5 Sastra of Maitreya
		Saraha's mystic songs
		Vajrayana meaning
	Khenchen Thrangu Rinpoché	Buddhist history
		Kagyu Indian hagiographies
		'Ornament of Liberation'
		Madhyamaka theory
		Mandalas and tormas
	Ven. Akong Rinpoché	teachings
1982	Khenpo Tsultrim Gyamtso	'Mahayana Sutralankara'
	Dilgo Khyentse Rinpoché	
	with accompanying tulkus	teachings & empowerments
		3-MONTH SUMMER SCHOOL
	the Goshir Gyaltsab	Mipam Rinpoché's 'Kenjuk' Bodhicaryavatara
	Ven. Akong Rinpoché	meditation/therapy
1983	the Goshir Gyaltsab	'Jewel Garland' by Gampopa
	Very Ven. Khenpo Kalu Rinpoché	teachings/empowerments
	Ven. Akong Rinpoché	meditation course
	Kenneth Holmes	Mahayana Uttara Tantra
	Khenchen Thrangu Rinpoché	Prajnaparamita/Tara
1984	Khenchen Thrangu Rinpoché	Nyungne Chenresi practice
	Khenchen Thrangu Rinpoché	3 yanas/Vajrayana retreat
	Dharmacarya Tenpa Negi	Tibetan grammar
	H.H. the Dalai Lama	teachings 'meaning of dharma' and 'mahayana'
	Dr. Ilham Trad	homeopathy
	Edith Irwin M.A.	therapy
	Kenneth Holmes	'Ornament of Liberation'
	Dolma Jeffreys	Tibetan art
	Ven. Lama Thubten	'Ocean of True meaning'
	Khenpo Tsultrim Gyamtso	samatta theory/3 yanas
1985	Ven. Akong Rinpoché	meditation/therapy

	Ven. Lama Pema Konchog	Tibetan art
	Ven. Akong Rinpoché	Buddhist approach to life/retreat
	Kenneth Holmes	'Ornament of Liberation'
	Ven. Lama Ganga	Kagyu hagiographies
	the Khentin Tai Situpa	**SUMMER SCHOOL**
		therapy/8 lineages
		mahamudra/death and dying
	Ven. Tulku Tenga	Vajrayana ritual/mandalas
1986	Ven. Tulku Tenga	astrology, medicine, Amitabha sadhana
	Kenneth Holmes	Mipam Rinpoché's 'Kenjuk'
	Peter Roberts	Tibetan language
	Ven. Akong Rinpoché	'Mahamudra's Ocean of True Meaning'
	Khenchen Thrangu Rinpoché	'Treasury of Knowledge'/ empowerments
	Ven. Akong Rinpoché	therapy
1987	Ven. Lama Namse	'Treasury of Knowledge'
	the Khentin Tai Situpa	'Treasury of Knowledge'/ empowerments
	Philip Johnson	'Bodhicaryavatara'
	Dr. Tashi Yengphel	Tibetan medicine/astrology
	Edith Irwin M.A.	'Taming the Tiger' therapy
	Peter Roberts	Tibetan language
	Kenneth Holmes	'Torch of Certainty'
	Ven. Akong Rinpoché	'Mahamudra's Ocean of True Meaning'
	Very Ven. Khenpo Kalu Rinpoché	Mahamudra/empowerments
	Ven. Akong Rinpoché	Therapy
	Lama Thubten	Taking Refuge: The Bodhisattva Vow
		Life of Khentin Tai Situ Pa
	Khentin Tai Situpa	Meditation Teaching: Shi Nay, Lhaktong,
		Maha, Vajra
	Kalu Rinpoché	Tun Shi Lami Naljor
		Yoga Exercises corresponding to Dharma
1988	Khentin Tai Situpa	Death & Dying, Mahamudra, Geomancy,
		Guru Rinpoche Teaching, Buddha's
		Teaching, Chod
	Kenchen Thrangu Rinpoché	3 Most Excellent Trainings of the Buddha
		Treasury of Knowledge (chapter 7)
		Shi Nay
		Guru Rinpoche Teaching
		Mahamudra
1989	Khentin Tai Situpa	Introduction to Mahamudra
	Ringu Tulku	She Sha Kun Kyab
	Akong Tulku Rinpoché	Foundations of Mahamudra
1990	Khenpo Tsultrim Gyamtso	Cho Nyi Nam Yed
	Akong Tulku Rinpoché	Nyung Nay Course
	Kenchen Thrangu Rinpoché	Intro.to Mahamudra Course
	Khentin Tai Situpa	Inauguration of Mani Wheel
		7 & 5 year course Mahamudra teachings

1991	Ringu Tulku	Lineage Teachings of Karma Kagyu
1992	Ringu Tulku	Introduction to Pey Cho Rinchen Pung Pa
		Pey Cho Rinchen Pung Pa
		General Talk on Buddhism
	Kenchen Thrangu Rinpoché	Talk on Mahamudra
	Akong Tulku Rinpoché	Therapy:Meditation Xmas Course
1993	HH Dalai Lama	"Inner Peace Leads to World Peace"
	Akong Tulku Rinpoché	Meditation
	Kenchen Thrangu Rinpoché	Talk on Mahamudra
	Khentin Tai Situpa	General Talk on Dharma
		7 & 5 year course Mahamudra teachings
1994	Ringu Tulku	Precious Rosary of Supreme Path(concise)
		Precious Rosary of Supreme Path
		Three Levels of Commitment
		Meditation Instructions
		Treasury of Knowledge (Chapters 1 to 4)
		Explanation of Green Tara Practice
		Explanation of Medicine Buddha Practice
		Explanation of Chenrezig practice
		Gampopa's Life Story
	Khenpo Troru Tsenam	Discerning Consciousness from Pure Awareness
	Akong Tulku Rinpoché	Meditation Talk
		Seven Points of Mind Training
	Khentin Tai Situpa	Role of Buddhism in Modern Life Today
		Buddhism in General
		Three Yanas of Buddhism
		Four Types of Buddhists
		Role of Buddhism in Modern Life Today
		Three Yanas of Buddhism
		Four Types of Buddhists
		7 & 5 year Mahamudra teachings
	Khenpo Troru Tsenam	Discerning Consciousness from Pure Awareness
		Nature of the Tathagatas
1995	Akong Tulku Rinpoché	Meditation Course
	Khenpo Troru Tsenam	Talk on Therapy
		Nature of the Tathagatas
	Ringu Tulku	Treasury of Knowledge
		Inspired Heart, Enlightened Mind
		Good in the Beginning, Middle &End (Patrul Rinpoche)
	Khentin Tai Situpa	Short Talk on Chö/Daily Chö Puja
		The Six Paramitas
		Talk on Buddhism

		Talk on Devotion
		The Six Paramitas
		Talk on Buddhism
		Talk on Devotion
		7 & 5 year Mahamudra teachings
1996	Ringu Tulku	Treasury of Knowledge
		Buddhist Outlook on Life
		Buddhism in Daily Life
	Khentin Tai Situpa	Talk on The Bardo
		Talk on Compassion & Bodhicitta
		Talk on Prajna Paramita
		Talk on The Five Skandhas/Refuge & Lineage
		Advice to Dharma Practioners
		Talks on Refuge & Lineage/Tara
		Talk on The Bardo
		Talk on Compassion
		The Prajna Paramita
		7 & 5 year course Mahamudra teachings
		Advice to Dharma Practioners
	Akong Tulku Rinpoché	Introduction to Easter Course
		Final Talk of Easter Course
		Green Tara Puja(Full version)
	Kenchen Thrangu Rinpoché	Teaching on Compassion
		Talk given to Sangha
		Teaching on Compassion
		Talk given to Sangha
1997	Akong Tulku Rinpoché	What is Buddhism/Meaning of taking Refuge(Interview)
		Milarepa Puja & Tsok Puja
	Khentin Tai Situpa	Talk on The Two Accumulations
		Talk on The Six Paramitas
		Talk on Purification
		Talk on Chö
		Talk on Chod: Meaning, Lineage, in Daily Life
		7 & 5 year course Mahamudra teachings
	Ringu Tulku	Treasury of Knowledge
	Lama Phuntsog	Explanation of Guru Rinpoche Initiation
		Explanation of Amitabha Initiation
		Talk on Stupas
	Sherab Palden	King Gesar of Ling Stories
1998	Lama Tenpa Gyaltsen	Voidness - The Middle Way
	Ringu Tulku	Treasury of Knowledge
		Series of Discussion, Q & A with Audience
	Ken Holmes	General Talk on Empowerments
		Talk on Buddha Nature
		Asanga's Uttara Tantra Sastra

	Akong Tulku Rinpoché	General Talk
1999	Akong Tulku Rinpoché	Community Talk at end of Nyung Neys
		Tara Praises/Mahamudra Prayer
	Ken Holmes	Talk on Mahamudra Prayer
		12 Major Events in the Buddha's Life
		12 Deeds of the Buddha
	Ringu Tulku	Treasury of Knowledge
		General Talks / Question & Answer Sessions
Khenpo Tsultrim Gyamtso		Mahasiddha Saraha and the Mahamudra Tradition
	Rob Nairn	Diamond Mind Part 1
2000	Ringu Tulku	Treasury of Knowledge
	Rob Nairn	Diamond Mind Part 2
2001	Ringu Tulku	Treasury of Knowledge
		The 4 Noble Truths
	Kenchen Thrangu Rinpoché	Karma Pakshi
		Bodhisattva Vow
2002	Akong Tulku Rinpoché	Reasons for Practice/How to develop a simple life
	Ringu Tulku	Treasury of Knowledge
	Kenchen Thrangu Rinpoché	Buddha's Teachings & Diligence
	Yongey Mingyur Dorje Rinpoche	Amitabha Buddha Teachings
2003	Ringu Tulku	Treasury of Knowledge
		The 4 Noble Truths
	Khenpo Tsultrim Gyamtso	"The Sun of Wisdom"
	Yongey Mingyur Dorje Rinpoché	Explanation of Bodhisattva Commitment & Vow
		Explanation of Vajrayana & Empowerments (Dorje Sempa)
		Kagyu Lineage / Guru Yoga
		Refuge & Dorje Sempa Practice
2004	Yongey Mingyur Dorje Rinpoché	Shiné and Lhaktong
		Dealing with the Emotions
		Mandala & Guru Rinpoche Prayers
	Ringu Tulku	Mahayana Philosophy and Practice
	Khenpo Tsultrim Gyamtso	Distinguishing Phenomena and Pure Being
	Ken Holmes	Identifying with Ultimate Truth
		Explanation of Refuge
	Lama Zangmo	Benefits of Green Tara Practice
	Lama Yeshe Rinpoche	Living Dharma
2004	Lama Yeshe Rinpoche	Better Living through Inner Strength

2005	Ringu Tulku	Meditation & Mahayana Buddhism
	Khenpo Tsultrim Gyamtso	The Moon of Wisdom
	Yongey Mingyur Dorje Rinpoché	Natural Peace
2006	Dulmo Chöje Rinpoche	Green Tara, Mahakala, and Guru Rinpoche
Pujas		
		Guru Rinpoche Drupchen
		Purba Drupchen on Holy Island
	Troru Tulku	Bodhisattva Path
		Jewel Rosary

Thanks to the dedicated work of Bill Trotter and Lorna Watson in Samye Ling's audio visual department many of these precious teachings have been recorded and are available on tape, video or DVD. A list of recorded teachings is available from the Samye Ling shop. Email: sales@samyelingshop.com

CHAPTER XVII

KAGYU SAMYE DZONGS,

ROKPA AND TARA ROKPA BRANCHES WORLD WIDE

Kagyu Samye Ling and its associated Centres worldwide all operate under the umbrella organization of the Rokpa Trust registered charity whose founder is Akong Tulku Rinpoche and whose President is Lama Yeshe Losal Rinpoche. Listed on the following pages are the names, addresses and contact numbers for all the Kagyu Samye Dzongs, Rokpa and Tara Rokpa branches around the world. The proliferation of these Centres speaks volumes about the influence that Kagyu Samye Ling has had in the spheres of charity, therapy and spirituality on a global level over the years. Time and space do not allow for detailed descriptions of all these branches. However, a few brief profiles are given featuring some of the the larger, long established Centres.

AFRICA

Akong Rinpoche's activity in Africa extends from Cape Town on the southern tip of the continent, north into the tropical jungle of the Democratic Republic of the Congo, although contact with the three Centres in the Congo has been sporadic since 1998 due to political problems. The Centres are focal points for all four aspects of Akong Rinpoche's work: Dharma, Tara Rokpa Therapy, Rokpa charity and preservation of the environment and wildlife. The Centres receive visits from Akong Rinpoche, Lama Yeshe Rinpoche and other respected Dharma and therapy teachers. Rob Nairn is Akong Rinpoche's main representative in Africa.

CAPE TOWN SAMYE DZONG

There have been various groups of Kagyu Buddhist practitioners in South Africa since the 1970's. One such group met in the home of Rob Nairn, who also established a retreat centre in Nieu Bethesda. After he had completed a 4 year retreat at Samye Ling Rob returned to Africa and, on the instruction of Akong Rinpoche, closed down the Nieu Bethesda centre when the first Cape Town Samye Dzong was bought in 1994. When the current Centre was acquired in 1999 a large shrine room was built to accommodate the growing number of practitioners. The Bardo group started in 2003 to promote awareness of the process of dying and death and how one may use one's life to positively prepare for death.
Tel +27 21 761 2978 capetown@kagyu.org.za

ROKPA CAPE MOUNTAIN RETREAT

This most recently established country Centre between the villages of Worcester and Villiersdorp - about two hours' drive from Cape Town was opened as an offering to Akong Rinpoche. After many years of searching a large, unspoilt property of 2300 acres, consisting mostly of rocky mountains, valleys and gorges was found two years ago. This was affordable and, with the help of a generous benefactor, is already bond free. The plan is to preserve the very special type of vegetation, known as renosterveld and to be as eco-friendly as possible with all development. Lama Yeshe Losal Rinpoche led a seven-day retreat in February 2007, which was a significant milestone for the centre and was attended by 70 people.
Tel +27 21 762 6210 Email caperetreat@kagyu.org.za

JOHANNESBURG SAMYE DZONG

Under the spiritual direction of Akong Rinpoche students established a Centre during the mid 1980s - later named the Johannesburg Samye Dzong. Since 1994 the Centre has been operating from its own premises in Kensington and now has Karma Shenpen as its resident monk. Situated at the top of a ridge, the Centre has a spacious view and provides a peaceful atmosphere. The three main aspects of Akong Rinpoche's teachings are presented, namely, spirituality, therapy and charity. A Rokpa soup kitchen was established in 1995 and provides food and clothing for homeless people in the inner city of Johannesburg. In 2004 an additional centre was started in **Randburg** - within the area of the city indicated by His Holiness the 17th Karmapa as being an auspicious place for a Centre nd in July 2005 a Dharma Group in neighbouring **Pretoria** was also started.
Tel + 27 11 614 1948 johannesburg@kagyu.org.za

GROOT MARICO TARA ROKPA HEALTHCARE CENTRE

This Centre is situated on 160 hectares of farmland in a beautiful, remote valley in the north western province of South Africa. Founded in 2002, it is headed by Akong Rinpoche. TRC is a Buddhist inspired Centre with a holistic approach to development for people of any or no faith, comprising four branches: (1) Dharma, with meditation courses and retreats; (2) Therapy, with Tara Rokpa therapy workshops as well as facilities rented out for other activities such as yoga courses; (3) Community project such as literacy programmes, skills development, training in eco-building; and (4) caring for and preserving the environment and wildlife.
Tel: + 27 14252 and ask for 1830 (shared land line)
trc@vodamail.co.za or trc@telkom.net

ROKPA ZIMBABWE - HARARE

Akong Rinpoche's first visit to Zimbabwe inspired the purchase of two acres of woodland near the Harare city centre in 1994. In 1998 more than 4 acres of land was bought on the hilltop above the existing Centre to become a city retreat. Houses for Akong Rinpoche and Rob Nairn were built, and in 2007 Lama Yeshe Rinpoche inaugurated the shrine room - the biggest Kagyu shrine room in Africa. There are two satellite Centres on the outskirts of Harare: **Chitungwiza Centre** has its own land and a rudimentary building while the **Dzivaresekwa** group operates in a private home. Akong Rinpoche urged Rokpa Harare to initiate dialogue with traditional spiritual leaders. Good relationships have been established with two eminent spirit mediums, one of whom, the Chaminuka medium, took refuge with Rinpoche and spearheaded the founding of the Chitungwiza Centre. Sadly, both the spirit mediums have since died. However, the spiritual foundation has been laid and is expressed in the dancing Chenrezig practice in Shona using traditional instruments. Rob Nairn's first book Tranquil Mind has been translated into a poetic Shona - Pfungwa Dzakagadzikana.

The humanitarian work of Rokpa Harare, supported by Rokpa International, is extensive. Projects include the promotion of small businesses for unemployed women, training in permaculture, upgrading squatter housing, providing medicines for the poor and HIV sufferers, and supplementary feeding of 400 families, mostly single mothers with disabled children.
Tel + 263 4 304 202 Email rokpa@mango.zw

BELGIUM
Kagyu Samye Dzong Brussels, Karma Shedrup Gyaltso Ling

During the first visit to the West of H.H. the 16th Gyalwa Karmapa, after having started the first Kagyu centre outside Samye Ling in Antwerp in 1974, Akong Rinpoche told students Carlo Luycx and Brigitte Cornelis to look for a place in Brussels, the capital of Europe, in preparation for the second visit of His Holiness in 1977. It was thus that a beautiful mansion house was found in the very centre of Brussels suitable for receiving His Holiness and his party for a week in July 1977 and for another week in November of the same year.

His Holiness appointed Akong Rinpoche as his representative and asked him to take responsibility for the centre, which Rinpoche did very skilfully, guiding the team of students who looked after the place over the last 30 years, visiting on a yearly basis and always making himself available for advice. The impressive house, built at the end of the 19th century with beautifully ornamented high ceilings was decorated in Tibetan style under the direction of Sherab Palden Beru. The spacious shrine room, blessed by visits from the highest Tibetan Lamas, was expanded in 2000 and features an intricately carved wooden shrine.

Many thousands of people have been able to make a connection with the precious Dharma, through seminars, meditation sessions and international congresses held at the Centre. Under the direction of Akong Rinpoche, a teaching programme over several years has given many people the possibility to get involved in the practice of Dharma in everyday life and in retreats. The Centre is currently run by Shenpen, who with his wife Zula, also manages Drupkang, a colourful shop which was opened on the premises in 2005 and now stocks a wide range of Buddhist books and artefacts, thus providing the Centre with an increased visibility and source of income.

The year 2007 is very auspicious since it marks not only the 40th anniversary of Kagyu Samye Ling but also the 30th anniversary of the Brussels Centre. Both of these events were celebrated with Akong Rinpoche who inaugurated the foundations of a Stupa in the garden, in the presence of the Minister-President of the Brussels Region and the Vice Prime Minister of Belgium, who announced that the Belgian Government has taken the first steps leading to the official recognition of Buddhism in Belgium. This historic occasion was followed by a Guru Rinpoche Drubcho with members of the Samye Ling Sangha leading the Centre's lay community in a meaningful and joyous seven day ceremony.

KSD Brussels, Karma Shedrup Gyamtso Ling, 33 Rue Capouillet, 1060 Bruxelles
Tel: +32 (0)2 5375407   Fax: +32 (0)2 5374245 centre@samye.be www.samye.be

KSD Nidrum, Auf dem Köttenberg, 14, 4750 Nidrum   Tel : +32 (0)80 44 76 36
Fax : +32 (0)80 44 87 46   dominiqv@euregio.net

CONGO (DRC)

KSD Lumbumbashi, c/o Francis Kyungu +24 3997024046 & 3997710456

CZECH REPUBLIC

KSD Plzen, c/o Dr. Helena Gajdosova, Raisova 21, Plzen 30100
Tel: +420 603 47 55 28   samyedzong@email.cz www.samye.aktualne.cz

GERMANY

KSD Kirchheim, Chang Chup Cho Ling, Alleenstraße 18, D 73230 Kirchheim unter Teck
Tel: +49 7021 58119   email petra.s@kirchheimsamye.org   www.kirchheim.samye.org

IRELAND

KSD Cork, "High Meadows", 6 Upper Panorama Terrace, Sunday's Well, Cork.

KSD Dublin

The Dublin Kagyu Samye Dzong Centre was founded in 1977 by a few Irish students of Buddhism who encountered Akong Rinpoche at the fledgling Samye Ling in Scotland. It was given the name *Dagpo Chökhor Ling* ('Gampopa's Dharma-wheel place') by H.H. Karmapa XVI and came under the aegis of Akong Tulku Rinpoche who was His Holiness, representative in Europe.

The Centre began without any material assets, sponsors or resources and its development over the years has been modest and measured. It was the first Buddhist organization of any tradition to be established in Ireland and so has been the setting for many 'first-time' Buddhist events in the country. H.E. Tai Situpa and H.E. Goshir Gyaltsab, the previous Kalu Rinpoche, Khenpo Tsultrim Gyamtso, Ringu Tulku and many other rinpoches, lamas, monks, nuns and lay teachers have stayed and taught at the Centre. Akong Rinpoche and Lama Yeshe Lösal Rinpoche have been frequent visitors. In its 21st year, the President of Ireland made an official call, probably the first visit by a European head of state to a European Buddhist centre.

The Centre now lives in a large Victorian house in one of the most historic areas of Dublin adjacent to Phoenix Park, with its herd of deer. The premises include a good-sized shrine room with a fine image of the Buddha, reception/lecture room, bookstall, visiting teachers' and other accommodation. The garden features a spring discovered by Akong Rinpoche, thought to be the latest incarnation of the ancient holy well of Kilmainham, lost for ninety years. The Centre is maintained by a registered charity, Kagyu Buddhism Ireland.

KSD Dublin, Kilmainham Well House, 56 Inchicore Road, Kilmainham, Dublin 8
Tel: +353 (0)1 453 7427   Fax: +353 (0)1 453 9312 info@buddhism.ie www.buddhism.ie

ITALY

KSD Venezia, Casella Postale 204 Venezia Centro, 30124 Venezia
tel. +39/328/2066438 www.samyedzongvenice.org info@samyedzongvenice.org

KSD Vicenza, Yoga Institute, Contra San Faustino 21, 36100 Vicenza
tel. +39/0444/381202   mahamudravicenza@libero.it

KSD Assisi, Via Baglioni 24, Petrignano d'Assisi (Pg)
tel. +39/393/3556140   mahamudraassisi@libero.it

KSD Padova, Selvazzano Dentro (Pd), Italy
tel. +39/347/4279214   mahamudrapadova@libero.it

KSD Rimini, Viale Baldini 15, Rimini   tel. +39/333/3733764, +39/339/6048241, +39/339/5674081   mahamudrarimini@libero.it

RUSSIA

KSD Moscow 30, 6/34 Pravdy Street, Moscow Tel: 8(910) 477-2138
www.karmakagyu.ru

SPAIN

Karma Lodro Gyamtso Ling – Samye Dzong Barcelona

In 1977 H.H. The 16th Gyalwa Karmapa gave his blessing and the name for the first Buddhist Centre in Spain to a group of young people who were students of Akong Rinpoche, whom he appointed as his representative in the whole country. The name he gave was Karma Lodro Gyamtso Ling, the karma place which is an ocean of intelligence. This was one of the first Samye Dzongs. Since then, some thirty years later this Centre, located in Barcelona, has grown and developed a few other Samye Dzongs, a Retreat Centre and meditation groups in other parts of Spain.

In 1993 Akong Rinpoche gave two fully ordained sangha members, a monk and a nun who had both completed two traditional four year retreats, the responsibility of running the Centre. In 2001 Rinpoche bestowed upon them the titles of Lama Jinpa Gyamtso and Lama Tsondru in recognition of their work as resident teachers in the Barcelona Centre in Barcelona and the other Samye Dzongs in Spain In 1994 the two Lamas started Samye Dzong Manresa, where a comfortable city centre apartment in the was bought in 1998 as a venue for dharma activities.

In 1996 some 80 acres of land with two farm houses were purchased in a mountainous region an hour and a half's drive from Barcelona. This became a retreat centre for weekend courses and summer retreats. However, in 2003 it was converted into a centre for strict retreats of long duration, and was subsequently closed to the public when a group of ten women and eight men started a three years and seven month retreat, the first of its kind to take place in Spain. The two Lamas share the job of instructing the retreatants while Akong Rinpoche and Lama Yeshe Losal Rinpoche visit them once a year. All the empowerments were given by Akong Rinpoche and Mingyur Rinpoche. This first long retreat will end in June 2007.

In 2002 the Lamas opened another Samye Dzong in Las Palmas, in the Canary Islands, where regular courses and activities have been taking place regularly in an apartment rented for the purpose. In 2005 a Dharma-study group was established in Madrid and another one in La Coruña, northwest Spain, both of which are visited regularly by the Lamas who give talks to a considerable number of people, although no fixed premises have been purchased yet.

Over the past thirty years a number of High Lamas and Rinpoches have visited the Centres, especially the main one in Barcelona, and have given teachings and initiations. Their Eminences Tai Situpa and Goshir Gyaltsab have visited as well as Kalu Rinpoche, Khenpo Tsultrim Gyamtso Rinpoche, Ringu Tulku Rinpoche, and Mingyur Rinpoche. Apart from continuing the activities in all the city Centres and in the Retreat Centre, the aim is to establish a new country Centre where short retreat and weekend courses can be given, and where individual people can do retreats of medium duration. This could also be a place where older people could retire in an atmosphere of Dharma practice and care. We hope this can become a monastery too, where ordained people can live and preserve the Dharma.

KSD Barcelona, Karma Lodro Gyamtso Ling, Rambla de la Muntanya, 97,
08041 Barcelona   Tel/Fax: +34 934362626
samyedzong@retemail.es   www.samye.org/spain

KSD Las Palmas, La Naval 184, 4°, 35008 Las Palmas Tel: +34 928 38 33 85
samyedzonglp@hotmail.com

KSD Manresa, Canonge Mulet, 2, 3°, 3ª, 08240 Manresa (Barcelona)
Tel: +34 93 872 0254

UNITED KINGDOM

HEADQUARTERS
Kagyu Samye Ling Monastery & Tibetan Centre, Eskdalemuir, Langholm,
Dumfriesshire DG13 0QL, Scotland   Tel: +44 (0)13873 73232
Fax: +44 (0)13873 73223   scotland@samyeling.org   www.samyeling.org

Kagyu Samye Dzong London

Kagyu Samye Dzong London is a branch of the world-renowned Kagyu Samye Ling monastery in Scotland. Situated in the heart of London just 5 minutes walk from the London Eye, it offers a unique place for people to unwind from the stressful pace of city life. The Centre has been open since 1998 and offers a varied programme of courses in meditation, Buddhism and related subjects. These courses are offered at low cost and use of the shrine room for personal practice and group meditation is free of charge. Due to the wishes and great interest shown by many people in London, Rokpa Trust was able to establish Kagyu Samye Dzong London which opened in April 1998. Under the spiritual guidance of Choje Akong Tulku Rinpoche, it has become one of the most successful city branches of Rokpa Trust, remaining open to the public more constantly than any other Centre. Samye Dzong is under the daily direction of Lama Zangmo, Rokpa's only western Lama in the UK, who has been fortunate enough to have the assistance of Ani Paltso a dedicated and hard-working nun, as well as many committed lay helpers. The Centre has been blessed over the years by the presence of many high Kagyu Lamas.
Kagyu Samye Dzong London, Carlisle Lane, Lambeth, London SE1 7LG
Tel: +44(0)207 928 5447 Fax:+44 (0)207 633 9339
www.samye.org/london   London@samye.org

Manor Place Samye Dzong London opened in March 2007. The beautiful 100-year old Victorian building was originally used by the local community as a Bath house and public laundry facility. It fell into disuse and has been rescued from the English Heritage 'buildings at risk' register by the impressive and fine workmanship of a dedicated team of Kagyu Samye Dzong London volunteers. Manor Place Samye Dzong is a part of Kagyu Samye Dzong London and presently gives the therapeutic side of Rokpa Trust's activities a real home in London. The Clinic is used each month by the visiting Tara Rokpa Tibetan Doctor, Dr. Lobsang

Dhonden. Many other professional therapists also practise from this new Centre. The rooms are available for hire and host a number of community orientated activities for people in the local area, and a constant programme of meditation courses and related activities are also organized by the Centre.

Manor Place Samye Dzong London, 33 Manor Place, London. SE17 3BD
Tel: +44(0)207 708 8969 www.london.samye.org london@samye.org

Rokpa Aberdeen, 6 Hosefield Road, Midstocket, Aberdeen AB15 5NB
Tel:+44 (0)7986 956365 info.rokpaaberdeen@gmail.com www.aberdeen.rokpa.org

Rokpa Cardiff, 100 Moorland Road, Cardiff CF24 2LP Tel: 02920 499185
(Lorraine Harris) info@rokpacardiff.com www.rokpacardiff.com

KSD Chichester, c/o Jill Domleo, Southern Comfort, West Bracklesham Drive, Bracklesham Bay, Chichester, W. Sussex PO20 8PF
Tel: +44 (0)1243 671309 Fax: 672872 chichester@samye.org

KSD Cornwall, c/o James Wainwright, Hedra, Genville Road,
Lostwithiel, Cornwall PL22 0EP Tel: +44 (0)1208 873785 pemawainwright@hotmail.com
http://groups.msn.com/KagyuSamyeDzongCornwall

Rokpa Dundee, 2nd Floor, 51 Reform Street, Dundee DD1 4NG
Tel: 01382 872020 Fax: 01382 872010 jiga@ecosse.net www.rokpa.org/dundee

KSD Edinburgh, c/o Paul Sode, paulsde@blueyonder.co.uk,
www.samyedzongedinburgh.org.uk

KSD Glasgow, 7 Ashley Street, Glasgow G3 6DR Tel: +44 (0)141 332 9950 Fax: +44 (0)141 429 0990 glasgow@rokpa.org www.rokpa.org/glasgow

The Holy Island Project

Located off the Ayrshire coastline in the Western Isles of Scotland, Holy Island has an ancient spiritual heritage and was the home of the 6th century Celtic Christian Sant Molaise who lived a life of spiritual seclusion in one of the island's caves. In 1992 the island was purchased by Rokpa Trust, after a determined fundraising drive headed by Lama Yeshe Losal Rinpoche, to be used as an ideal place for retreat and health promoting activities open to people of all faiths. The dedicated efforts of resident and visiting volunteers transformed the semi-derelict buildings at the north and the south ends of the island into comfortable and attractive accommodation. Wherever possible, ecologically sound materials and methods were used, including non-toxic, bio-degradable paint and environmentally friendly insulation materials. Care for the environment has always been an important part the Holy Island ethos. More than 35.000 native Scottish trees have been planted and are monitored as part of the ongoing environmental work carried out on the island. The rich abundance of wild life has also been helped by cutting down large areas of bracken to allow grass to grow and nourish the rare breeds of wild Eriskay ponies, Soay sheep and Sanaan goats, all of whom supplement their diet with nutritious seaweed and are thriving, as are the islands' many species of birds.

Since 1995, long term Buddhist retreats have taken place at the south end of the island in the beautifully renovated Lighthouse Cottages. In March 2006 the first traditional three years and three months retreat for women was successfully completed by an international group of twelve women. And in 2003 the Centre for World Peace and Health opened at the north end of the island, providing the ideal venue for a programme of courses and short retreats. The Centre is open to people of all faiths and none. Courses include Meditation, Yoga, Tai Chi, Interfaith Dialogue, Gardening, Cooking and many other topics that contribute to peace and well-being. Overnight guests are welcome to stay at the centre all year round in comfortable has guest house facilities. Day visitors are also welcome to enjoy the unspoiled beauty of the island and visit the sacred sites. The Centre is available for hire by groups of all faiths, by complementary health practitioners and by any other organisations that respect the islands' Five Golden Rules. Individual guests can also stay at the Centre, which provides accommodation for over 60 people in a range of single, twin and dormitory rooms.

Holy Island Project, Centre for World Peace and Health, Holy Island, Lamlash Bay, Isle of Arran, KA27 7GB   Tel:+44 (0)1770 601100   reception@holyisland.org www.holyisland.org

KSD Highland, c/o Connie McCreath 26 Red Craig Forres
Morayshire IV36 2JR   tel: 01309 673529

Rokpa Highlands, c/o Hazel Young, 20 Lodgehill Park, Nairn IV12 4SB
+44 (0)1667 453413 hazely@btopenworld.com

KSD Northamptonshire, Friends Meeting House, Northall Street, Northants NN16 8DS
tel: +44 (0)7812567496   kettsamyedzong@aol.com www.samyedzongnorthants.org

KSD Sandhurst, c/o Joy Godfrey, 2, Lamborne Close, Scotland Hill,
Sandhurst, Berkshire GU47 8JL
Tel: +44 (0)1344 762392   sandhurst@samye.org

UK Samye Practice Groups

Brighton Green Tara c/ Patricia Whiting, Flat 3, 20 Cambridge Rd, Hove,
E. Sussex BN3 1DF Tel: +44 (0)1273 739187 greentara-brighton@amserve.com

High Peak, c/o Sarah Lionheart, Tel: 01663 732 701sarah@heartandmind.org

Northumberland, c/o Gwennie Fraser Tel: (01434) 220647gwennie.fraser@zen.co.uk

ROKPA - HUMANITARIAN AID

ROKPA INTERNATIONAL HEADQUARTERS
Böcklinstrasse 27, 8032 Zurich, Switzerland
Tel: +41 (0)44 262 6888, Fax: +41 (0)44 262 6889, info@rokpa.ch www.rokpa.org

The Worldwide ROKPA Partnership

AUSTRIA
ROKPA Oesterreich, Dipl.-Ing. Eric Leitner, Stutz 81, A-6888 Schröcken,
Tel: +43 (0)34 79280   rokpa-austria@gmx.at   www.rokpa.at

BELGIUM

ROKPA Belgium a.s.b.l.v.z.w., c/o Vinciane Debruyne, 33, Rue Capouillet, 1060 Bruxelles.
Telefax: +32 (0)2 538 13 80 vinciane@rokpa.be www.rokpa.be
ROKPA Antwerp c/o Eva Sculsky, Kreeftstraat 28, 2018 Antwerpen
Tel: +32 (0)3 272 01 91 ropa.vzw@antwerpen.be

CANADA

ROKPA Canada, 212-2678 West Broadway, Vancouver BC, V6K 2G3
Tel:+1 (0)604 733 1055, Fax: +1 (0)604 732 6809 charitable reg. 926 212 09
rokpaca@telus.net www.rokpa.ca

FINLAND

ROKPA Finland, c/o Ani Sherab, Marunakuja 6 A 2, 00840 Helsinki
Tel: +358 (0)40 7022979 rokpa@rokpafinland.org www.rokpafinland.org

FRANCE

ROKPA France, c/o Françoise Prudhomme, 11, rue des Boulangers
75005 Paris Tel: +33 (0)1 43 54 14 32 Fax: +33 (0)1 44 27 59 67
francoise.prudhomme@snv.jussieu.fr www.rokpa-france.org

GERMANY

ROKPA Deutschland e.V., Info-Burö-Konstanz, Anja Hufer, Scheffelstr. 6, D-78462
Konstanz Tel: +49 (0)7531 916540 info@rokpa-deutschland.de www.rokpa-deutschland.de

HOLLAND

ROKPA Holland, c/o Pim Willems, Hartmanstraat 12, NL-2313 NB Leiden, Tel: +31 (0)71
5123 552 rokpa@tiscali.nl www.rokpa.nl

INDIA

ROKPA Charitable Society c/o Dr S Khedup, Shambala House No 27, New Aruna Nagar,
Manjuka Tilla, Delhi 110094 khedup_hma@hotmail.com
ROKPA SIKKIM, c/o Ringu Tulku, Rigul House, Secretariat Rd, Gangtok, Sikkim 737103

IRELAND

ROKPA AID (Ireland) Ltd, c/o Pat Murphy, Coillbeg, Kylebeg, Blessington, Co. Wicklow
Tel: +353 (0)1473 1223 pat.murphy@qub.ac.uk

ITALY

Rokpa Italia, Casella Postale 137, 36100 Vicenza, tel. +39 3339753088+39 049661118
www.rokpaitalia.it info@rokpaitalia.it

NEPAL

ROKPA NEPAL, ROKPA House   Tel. +977 1 4 470594, mail: ROKPA Chidren's Home, P O Box 85, Boudhanath, KathmanduFax: +9771 471 902   email: rokpa@wlink.com.np
N.B. Fax (always write:"For ROKPA House, Tel: 470 594")

POLAND

ROKPA Polska, c/o Grzegorz Bral, Anna Zubrzycki, ul. Chorzowska 2/4, 52-023 Wroclaw,
Tel: +48 (0)71 340 07 51 or +48 (0)60 340 15 60   songofthegoat@poczta.onet.pl

SOUTH AFRICA

ROKPA Capetown, c/o Kagyu Samye Dzong, 6 Morgenrood Road, Kenilworth 7708,
Capetown   Tel: +27 (0)21 761 29 78   samye@absamail.co.za www.rokpa.co.za

ROKPA Johannesburg, 43 Floss Street, Kensington 2094
+27 (0)11 614 1948   dorje@gem.co.za www.rokpa.co.za

SPAIN

Fundacion ROKPA (Barcelona), c/o Rita Sagarra & Ignasi Caño, C/ Galicia, 3, E-08107
Martorelles, Telefax: +34 (0)93 579 17 31   ritaignasi@yahoo.es

ROKPA Euskadi, c/o Katalina Eleizegi 38, bajo, E-20009 Donostia (Gipuzkoa)   Tel: +34 (0)943 473815, rokpaeusk@euskalnet.net   www.la-concha.com/rokpa

ROKPA España (Madrid), Aitor Rey Guenaga, c/Maestro Alonso 13, 4°-2a Madrid 28028
Tel.:   +34 (0)91 361 12 21   aitorrokpa@terra.es

ROKPA España (Manresa), Encarna Sanchez, C/ Canonge Mulet no 2, 3° - 3a, E-08240
Manresa (Barcelona), Tel: +34 (0)93 872 0254   rokpa.manresa@hotmail.com

Fundación ROKPA (Galicia), Luis Alberto Fernández Viz, C/ Pintor Laxeiro no 1, 5A° - izq.,
E-36500 Lalín (Pontevedra), Tel: +34 (0)986 78 34 52   rokpa_g@hotmail.com

Fundación ROKPA (Islas Canarias), Alejandro Torrealba Álvarez, "Centro Milarepa", La Naval, 167, 2°, E-35008 Las Palmas de Gran Canaria, Tel: +34 (0)928 460 864
cmilarepa@auna.com

Fundació ROKPA Mollet, C/ Jordi Rebull Isern, Berenguer III, 3 E-08100 Mollet del Vallés (Barcelona), Tel: +34 (0)93 579 22 08   rebull.planella@terra.es

Fundación ROKPA (Granollers y Baix Maresme), Lidia Montsant Damia, C/ de l'església antiga, 14, 2° - 1a, E-08392 Sant Andreu de Llavaneres (Barcelona).
Tel: +34 (0)93 792 6562   rokpa.gra@terra.es

SWITZERLAND

ROKPA SWITZERLAND
Böcklinstrasse 27, 8032 Zurich, Switzerland   Tel: +41 (0)44 262 6888,
Fax: +41 (0)44 262 6889,   info@rokpa.ch   www.rokpa.ch

UNITED KINGDOM

ROKPA Aberdeen, c/o Steve Hardie, 1st Floor Flat, 32 Hollybank Place, Aberdeen, AB11 6XS, Tel:+44 (0)7986 956365   steve.hardie@foodstuffs.gsi.gov.uk

ROKPA Dundee, 51 Reform Street, Dundee DD1 1SL, Tel: +44 (0)13828 72020
Fax:+44 (0)1382 87201info@dundee.rokpa.org   www.rokpa.org/dundee

ROKPA UK Overseas Projects, Kagyu Samye Ling, Eskdalemuir, Langholm, Dumfriesshire DG13 0QL   Tel: +44 (0)13873 73232 ext 30
Fax: +44 (0)13873 73340   charity@rokpaUK.org   www.rokpaUK.org

ROKPA Glasgow, 7 Ashley Street, Woodlands, Glasgow G3 6DR
Tel: +44 (0)141 429 0300   Fax: +44 (0)141 429 0990
glasgow@rokpa.org   www.rokpa.org/glasgow

U. S. A.

ROKPA USA, c/o Edith Irwin or Virginia Dempsey, 6501 Gretna Green Way
Alexandria VA, 22312 USA   Tel +1 703 642 2248 Fax +1 703 642 1591
rokpa.usa@attglobal.net   www.rokpausa.org   (federal ID# 31-1331706)
U.S.A. Regional contacts:
CALIFORNIA   Sylvia Timbers, P.O. Box 888, Inverness CA 94937
Tel: +1 415 663 1101   stimbers@earthlink.net
COLORADO   Rick DeSelm, Box 1738, Telluride CO 81435
Tel: +1 970 728 5108   rickdeselm2000@yahoo.com

ZIMBABWE

ROKPA Zimbabwe, c/o Trish Swift & Jane Soper, 34/31 Quendon Road, Monavale, Mabelreign, Harare Tel: +263 4 304411 Fax: +263 4 304202 rokpa@mango.zw

TARA ROKPA THERAPY

International HQ

TARA ROKPA, 84A Trees Rd., Mount Merrion, Co. Dublin, Ireland
Tel: +353 (0)1 278 8897   taratrt@eircom.net

Tara Institute of Tibetan Medicine, Dr. Lobsang Dhonden,

Tara Rokpa Edinburgh, 15 Rosebery Crescent, EH12 5JY   Tel: +44 (0)131 313 0304
tararokpa@tiscali.co.uk

Lothlorien Therapeutic Community

Lothlorien is a therapeutic community for people with mental health problems. It is situated in a quiet rural setting in South West Scotland. Buddhist values of compassion and tolerance are the basis of the approach, but it is not a religious community and is open to everyone.

Over the years, many people with mental health problems had sought the support of the Samye Ling community and by the mid 1980s efforts were being made to find a suitable setting in which to offer more specialist support. This came to fruition in 1989, when The Rokpa Trust acquired Lothlorien. The 13 bedroom log house, one of the largest in its kind in Britain, was built from locally hewn larch and pine trees. The house has places for 8 people with mental health problems and 4 voluntary co-workers, who live as part of the community in a supportive, befriending role. The 4 staff, known as the Core Group, comes in on weekdays.

The community has 17 acres including organic vegetable gardens, woodland, an orchard and willow beds. The practical tasks of community life, such as gardening, cooking and cleaning, have a grounding effect and the rhythm of daily life provides a structure which helps to restore a sense of balance to people's lives. The main focus is on the vegetable garden which provides enough for the community to be mostly self- sufficient for 4 months of the year.

As a therapeutic community, Lothlorien aims to help people to develop their strengths and to work towards recovery through the shared experience of community life. It differs from the usual approach to residential care by minimising the distinctions between staff, volunteers and residents and avoids the division between those who are 'well' providing care for those who are 'unwell'. Instead, the aim is to create a culture of mutual support, which helps people to develop their strengths and allows them to see themselves as having something to offer as well as having something to gain from community life.

Central to the life of the community is the daily meeting, where work and other activities are planned, decisions made and any issues of living together as a group in an open way are addressed. The weekly programme also includes methods based on the Tara Rokpa Therapy process such as relaxation, art therapy and massage. There are also regular Tai Chi classes.

People come to Lothlorien from all over the UK and are usually funded by their local social services. The maximum stay is 2 years. Most community members report a significant difference in the quality of their lives as a result of their time at Lothlorien. Generally, people find that living as part of a therapeutic community has lead to an increased self-awareness and a confidence in relating to others. The daily routine helps people to rebuild their lives and has been shown to be a good foundation for moving onto employment, education or training.

A second house, Roan Lodge, opened in 2003. It is situated near the main house at Lothlorien and provides accommodation for 5 people. It aims to help people regain an independent lifestyle, while continuing to receive the support of being connected to Lothlorien Community. At Roan Lodge, community members can pursue outside interests with a greater freedom. There is an expectation to do a certain amount of work in the communal vegetable gardens every week. However, the overall focus is on a greater interaction with the wider community as a means to develop more independence and autonomy.

Lothlorian Corsock, Castle Douglas, Dumfriesshire DG7 3DR
Tel: +44 (0)1644 440602

Tara Rokpa Therapy Trainers/Therapists

Dorothy Gunne, M.A., M.Psych.Sc.(Psychotherapy).,A.P.Ss.I.
84, Trees Road, Mount Merrion, Co.Dublin, Ireland
Tel: +353-1 275 5100 dot.gunne@eircom.net

Edie Irwin, M.A., EAP TRT, UKCP,Tara Rokpa Edinburgh, 15 Rosebery Crescent, EH12 5JY
Tel: +44 (0)131 225 6928   edietre@toucansurf.com

Dr Brion Sweeney, M.B., M. Med.Sc.(Psychotherapy), M.R.C. Psych.
84A Trees Road, Mount Merrion, Co.Dublin, Ireland   Tel: +353 (0)1 278 8897
tatatrt@eircom.net

Trish Swift, B.Soc.Sc., M.S.S., M.Sc., Rokpa Zimbabwe, 34 Quendon Road, Monavale, PO
Mabelreign, Harare, Zimbabwe
Tel: +263 4 304411 Fax: +263 4 722957   trishrokpa@zol.co.zw

Tara Rokpa Therapists

S E Atkin, Dip.Ed, 7 Ryehill Park, Eskdalemuir, Dumfriesshire DG13 0QF
Scotland, UK   Tel: +44 (0)13873 73222   info@susanatkin.co.uk

 Annie Dibble, B.A., IAHIP,TRT EAP, Tel: +353 (0)87 286 1090   annietrt@eircom.net

Heather Dudley, BA Hons, Dip AT, Dip Psychotherapy, 12 Douglas Crescent,
Gelston, Castle Douglas, Kircudbrightshire, DG7 1SJ, Scotland, UK
Tel: +44 (0)1556 502482   heather.dudley@phonecoop.coop

Lorna Hensey, BSoc. SC.,TRT UKCP, Netherbar Croft, Corsock, Castle Douglas,
Kirkcudbrightshire, DG7 3DT Scotland, UK.
Tel +44 (0)1644 440 280   lornahensey@btopenworld.com

Carol Phelan, BSc, (H Psych), Dip SW, IAHIP, Dunmore Lane, Falcarragh,
Co Donegal, Ireland   Tel: +353 (0)74 35022   Carol.Phelan@eircom.net

Stephan Storm, Dipl-Psych., Harkortsieg 4, 22765 Hamburg, Germany
Mobile: +49 (0)173 3778968   stormtrt@aol.com

Claudia Wellnitz,Via Stazione 13a, 39052 Caldaro, Italy
Tel/Fax +39 (0)471 964183   c.well@iol.it

Tara Rokpa Contacts

France
Marie-France Kunlin, 11 Rue Baillou, 75014 Paris. Tel: +33 1 454 23833
mfkunlin@hotmail.com

Germany
Petra Niehaus (see below)

Italy
Claudia Wellnitz, Bahnhofstr 13a, 39052 Kaltern, Italy
Tel/Fax +39 (0)471 964183   c.well@iol.it

Poland
c/o Grzegorz Bral, Anna Zubrzycki, ul. Chorzowska 2/4,
52-023 Wroclaw, Tel: +48 -71 3418488   office@piesnkozla.art.pl

South Africa
Sharon Benatar, 43 Floss Street, Kensington 2094
Tel: +27 (0)11 614 1948   dorje@gem.co.za

Sweden
Rosemary Renshaw, Pema Hvb, Larum2, Gamleby, 59492 Sweden
Tel: +46 (0)493 34003   pemahvb@telia.com

United Kingdom
General Coordinator:
Soo Dawson, BSc, Cert.Ed., 22 Manston Road, Exeter EX1 2QA UK
Tel: +44 (0)1392 668651   SooDawson@aol.com

Coordinator, Germany
Tara Rokpa Deutschland, c/o Petra Niehaus, Gartenstr. 48
52064 Aachen, Tel: +49 (0)241 872453   Fax +49 (0)241 876441
info@tararokpa.de   Web: www.tararokpa.de

IN CONCLUSION

THANKS TO ALL SAMYE LING'S SUPPORTERS

It was Akong Tulku Rinpoche's wish to conclude this 40th anniversary book with a list of all the people who have contributed their time, skills and/or funds to Samye Ling during the last forty years. On reflection, it soon became apparent that such a list would consist of thousands of names, take months to research and would in all probability be longer than the rest of the book put together. It would have resulted in a telephone directory sized tome.

However, Akong Tulku Rinpoche and Lama Yeshe Losal Rinpoche would like to extend their heart felt thanks to every single person who has helped Samye Ling, and all its associated Projects, grow from modest beginnings to the world renowned organisation it is today. Whether your contribution was £1 or £100,000, whether you worked for four days or forty years, in an office or a kitchen, cooking, gardening, cleaning, building, writing, teaching, however you helped, every one of you has contributed to the success of Samye Ling.

By pooling our energy and resources we have created a Monastery and Tibetan Centre truly worthy of the name Samye Ling, a place where precious Buddhadharma is preserved and practised for the benefit of all beings, a thriving community based on altruistic ideals and an oasis of peace and calm where people of all faiths are welcome to participate in the many wholesome activities on offer.

This book was commissioned and written in gratitude to everyone who has helped make Samye Ling what it is today, with the sincere wish that you receive all the blessings and merit you so richly deserve.